COMPREHENSIVE ASSURANCE
&
SYSTEMS TOOL

An Integrated Practice Set

THIRD EDITION

LAURA R. INGRAHAM
SAN JOSE STATE UNIVERSITY

J. GREGORY JENKINS
VIRGINIA POLYTECHNIC INSTITUTE AND STATE UNIVERSITY

ASSURANCE MODULE

PEARSON

Boston   Columbus   Indianapolis   New York   San Francisco   Upper Saddle River

Amsterdam   Cape Town   Dubai   London   Madrid   Milan   Munich   Paris   Montreal   Toronto

Delhi   Mexico City   Sao Paulo   Sydney   Hong Kong   Seoul   Singapore   Taipei   Tokyo

We dedicate this book to our families:
Dan and Casey
Elaine, Anna, Claire and Will

Editor in Chief: Donna Battista
Director, Product Development: Ashley Santora
Acquisitions Editor: Victoria Warneck
Editorial Project Manager: Christina Rumbaugh
Editorial Assistant: Jane Avery and Lauren Zanedis
Director of Marketing: Maggie Moylan Leen
Marketing Manager: Alison Haskins
Marketing Assistant: Kimberly Lovato
Production Manager: Meghan DeMaio
Cover Designer: Suzanne Behnke
Cover Image: Fotolia
Printer/Binder: LSC Communications
Cover Printer: LSC Communications

Credits and acknowledgments borrowed from other sources and reproduced, with permission, in this textbook appear on appropriate page within text.

Many of the designations by manufacturers and seller to distinguish their products are claimed as trademarks. Where those designations appear in this book, and the publisher was aware of a trademark claim, the designations have been printed in initial caps or all caps.

Library of Congress Cataloging-in-Publication Data is available.

11

ISBN 10: 0-13-309921-0
ISBN 13: 978-0-13-309921-8

Table of Contents

Assurance Module

Preface

The **C**omprehensive **A**ssurance and **S**ystems **T**ool (CAST) provides an integrated learning opportunity that encompasses financial statement assurance and accounting information systems. CAST uniquely exposes students to these issues at The Winery at Chateau Americana, a hypothetical company that is based on an actual domestic winery. Unlike traditional projects and assignments that may offer little or no context, students develop a rich knowledge and understanding of Chateau Americana and its industry as they provide assurance on the company's financial statements and address a variety of challenging accounting information systems issues.

CAST is comprised of three self-contained, but complementary modules:

- The *Manual AIS module* requires students to complete real-world business documents, journalize and post a variety of transactions, and prepare a year-end worksheet. The module now contains three alternative transaction sets to allow the instructor to rotate through them from semester to semester and to afford some variety among the transactions provided. This module may be completed before or during the completion of either the Computerized Accounting Information Systems module or the Assurance module. However, students are not required to complete this module before the other modules.
- The *Computerized Accounting Information Systems module* is comprised of three components: spreadsheets, general ledger software, and databases. Each of these components may be completed individually. However, the module itself is written so that each component strengthens the knowledge learned in the previous component. In addition, although self-contained, this module's value is greatest when combined with the Manual AIS module.
- The *Assurance module* provides students hands-on experience with fundamental elements of financial statement assurance. This module is comprised of components related to the client acceptance decision, understanding the business environment, understanding and testing internal controls, assessing risks and materiality, conducting substantive tests, evaluating attorney's letters, performing analytical review procedures, and determining the appropriate audit opinion. These components build upon one another and should be completed in the order in which they are presented.

CAST should be implemented in either an undergraduate or graduate setting and is ideally suited for simultaneous integration across assurance and information systems courses. In addition, each of the modules can be completed either as an in-class or an out-of-class assignment. CAST affords students the opportunity to develop and strengthen their analytical thinking, written and oral communication, problem solving, and team building skills.

The third edition has been updated in response to the changes that have occurred in the accounting environment, in technology, and in response to the many helpful comments and suggestions we have received from adopters and students alike. Specifically, we have incorporated new transactions in the Manual Module that are intended to reinforce more advanced accounting transaction processing. In the Computerized AIS Module, we have provided more advanced Macro instruction and additional PivotTable practice. And, in the Assurance Module we have updated materials for changes in professional standards and introduced new audit issues for students to address related to conflicting client inquiry and misstatements. We are excited about the changes we have made to this 3rd edition. We believe your students will benefit from using CAST and we once more encourage you to contact us with questions or suggestions about how we can improve the materials.

Finally, we would like to thank Monica Horenstein for her many hours spent checking and editing these Modules. Her contribution was invaluable.

Laura Ingraham
Greg Jenkins

CLIENT ACCEPTANCE:
The Winery At Chateau Americana

LEARNING OBJECTIVES

After completing and discussing this case, you should be able to:

- Understand types of information used to evaluate a prospective audit client
- Evaluate background information about an entity and key members of management
- Perform and evaluate preliminary analytical procedures
- Make and justify a client acceptance decision
- Describe matters that should be included in an engagement letter

INTRODUCTION

Since its founding in 1980, Chateau Americana (CA) has cultivated a reputation as one of America's finest wineries. The small, family-owned winery has an impressive vineyard whose 125 acres yields a variety of grapes including Cabernet Sauvignon, Cabernet Franc, Chardonnay and Riesling. In the last several years, CA's wines have received accolades at several highly regarded wine competitions which have dramatically increased the demand for its wines. This recent growth, along with the accompanying challenges and opportunities, has caused the winery's management to have doubts as to whether their current accounting firm is prepared to provide the advice and services required by a growing company.

Claire Helton, a partner with your accounting firm (Boston & Greer, LLP) recently met with the winery's president and chief financial officer (CFO) about the company's present and future needs. After several follow-up meetings, the winery's CFO contacted Claire to notify her that CA would like to have your firm submit a proposal to perform the company's financial statement audit. You have been asked by Claire to assist her in the evaluation of CA as a potential audit client and to assist with the preparation of the engagement proposal.

BACKGROUND INFORMATION

CA, owned by the Summerfield family, is a relatively modest winery with an annual production of approximately 385,000 cases of wine. Several years of sales growth have enabled the company to reinvest in its operations while simultaneously reducing its debts. Encouraged by its success and growing acclaim, management is contemplating an initial public offering within the next several years.

Overview of the Wine Industry

The domestic wine industry is comprised of almost 1,800 wineries. California is home to more than 800 of these wineries, almost half of the nation's wineries. More impressive still, California wineries account for more than 90 percent of the annual domestic wine production (565 million gallons) and approximately 70 percent of the nation's $19 billion in sales. An understanding of California's wineries is instructive because it is a "snapshot" of the domestic wine industry. The wine industry is highly concentrated with the five largest US winemakers accounting for 55 percent of domestic wine production.

Several of the world's largest winemakers are located in California. Ernest & Julio Gallo, one of the largest winemakers in the world, is privately owned and is estimated to have annual sales in the billions of dollars. Another large winemaker, one that is publicly-owned, is Constellation Brands. The company has seen its annual sales vary between $2.9 and $4.8 billion. Although there are several other large California wineries, they are much smaller than Gallo and Constellation with annual sales that are generally less than $200 million. In addition, many small California wineries specialize in the production of particular varieties of grapes and generate much lower sales.

Wine reaches the consumer through a variety of distribution channels. More than 43 percent of wine sales occur through supermarket chains. Specialty shops and mass merchandisers account for 24 percent and 19 percent of sales, respectively. The remainder is accounted for by restaurants, small convenience stores, and other outlets. Internet sales and distribution are relatively small primarily because of financial security concerns and interstate alcohol shipping regulations.

The wine industry appears to have a bright future. Wine consumption is directly related to household income, with higher income families consuming more wine than lower income families. Consumption is highest among adults between the ages of 35 and 64 because of higher disposable income. An aging and prosperous baby boom generation is expected to increase wine consumption and support premium priced wines. Consolidation within the industry is likely to continue as wineries search for economies of scale in production and advertising and interest in product expansion (i.e., grape varieties and brand names) broadens.

Overview of Chateau Americana

CA has experienced significant sales growth in recent years and expects to report record sales of almost $22 million for the year ending December 31, 20XX. Audited sales for the two prior years totaled $20.2 and $18.2 million, respectively. Over the same three year period, the company's asset base has also grown, increasing by more than 15 percent from $36.4 to $42 million. CA has been a profitable winery for a number of years and expects to report profits of approximately $2 million for the current year. Much of CA's growth has been fueled through the company's policy of reinvestment. To this end, retained earnings have increased approximately $3.7 million over the last three years, while total liabilities have increased $1.9 million. The winery's CFO provided the balance sheets and income statements for the current and two preceding years which are presented at the end of this narrative.

The winery's crown jewel is its 125-acre vineyard which yields a harvest of some fifteen varieties of grapes. Each year the vineyard provides approximately 800 tons of grapes, or one-fourth of the winery's production requirement. The remaining grapes are purchased from other vineyards, most of which are in California. CA is particularly proud of its production process - a blend of traditional techniques and state-of-the-art technology – which produces widely acclaimed red and white wines.

The company primarily sells its wines to distributors and retail shops. CA has developed several exclusive distribution agreements which have significantly increased its presence in several large metropolitan areas. The company is seeking similar opportunities in other areas.

The Company's Management

CA has a management team that is widely respected in the industry. The winery's owners have invested considerable time and energies in hiring individuals whom they believe are competent and trustworthy. Several members of the Summerfield family occupy key management positions.

- Edward Summerfield is the family's patriarch and president of the company. He has received several entrepreneurship awards and is generally perceived as an astute business person.
- Taylor Summerfield is vice president of marketing for the company. Prior to assuming this position, she had a successful career in sales and marketing. Taylor is well-educated and earned an MBA from an Ivy League school.
- Jacques Dupuis, Edward's son-in-law, is vice-president of winery operations. He has an extensive background in viticulture (i.e., grape growing) and vinification (i.e., wine making).
- Rob Breeden, the company's CFO, is the sole individual to hold a key management position who is not a member of the Summerfield family. He has substantial financial experience and was previously employed in public accounting for nine years and served as controller and CFO for another winery in California. Rob holds undergraduate and graduate degrees in accounting and is a CPA.

Edward and other members of management have taken considerable steps to ensure the stability of the winery's management team. To this end, management members have an open door policy that encourages a free exchange of ideas and concerns. In addition, Edward has instituted a compensation plan that provides substantial bonuses to all employees, including members of management, who meet performance goals. He believes that his policies and approach to business are the reasons that CA has had very low employee turnover. In fact, Rob is the newest member of management with just over two years of service to the company. He replaced the former CFO who resigned from the company after more than 15 years. According to Edward, the former CFO resigned because he wanted to spend more time with his wife who was suffering from a serious illness.

Client Background Investigation

Your firm customarily has a background investigation conducted prior to accepting a new audit client. The investigation of CA included the winery's corporate history and the background of each member of management. Two issues arose during the investigation. First, the company's credit history indicates that the company was delinquent on several obligations that were referred to collection agencies six years ago. Recent credit history is much more favorable and no problems of ongoing significance were found. The second issue relates to criminal charges filed against Jacques Dupuis while living in France. According to public records and news sources, Jacques and several other employees were accused of stealing trade secrets from a former employer – a French winery. Although charges were eventually dropped because of insufficient evidence, many in France still believe Jacques was guilty of stealing trade secrets.

The Company's Information System

The winery employs a fully integrated information system (IS) to collect, store and share data among its employees. The present system has been operational for approximately 14 months. Although employees are generally satisfied with the system, some complain that the transition from the previous system occurred too quickly and without adequate planning and training. Although the company has been computerized for more than 10 years, its former system was a combination of manual and computerized processes. Consequently, the new system represents a significant change in the company's IS.

Management believes the new system is the best on the market. After having been through a similar IS conversion process at his former employer, Rob Breeden insisted that the company investigate the prospects of developing an integrated IS using database technology. Following his detailed evaluation of the potential for in-house development of the system, Rob advised Edward that the system could be developed by the company's employees. Internal memos obtained from the company indicate that Edward deferred to Rob's judgment in making the decision to proceed with the in-house development process.

The current system is based on a relational database. The IS modules include purchasing and accounts payable, sales and accounts receivable, production and inventory, payroll, and the general ledger. Each of these modules provides data that are critical to the company's continued growth and success. Internal memos indicate that the company has experienced some employee turnover because of continuing problems with the accounts payable and accounts receivable modules. In fact, there are rumors that the former CFO resigned over disagreements with Edward about the need for a new IS.

Discussions with the Predecessor Auditor

As required by auditing standards, your firm asked for and received permission from management to contact the company's former auditor. Several phone calls were required before you were able to speak with the former partner-in-charge of the CA audit, Harry Lawson. At first, Harry was hesitant to talk with you about his firm's past relationship with CA. He said he needed to speak with Rob Breeden before you and he could have any substantive conversation.

You met with Harry at his office a few days later to learn more about his firm's relationship with the winery's management and recent audits. Harry was very complementary of the Summerfield family, describing Edward as a man of great integrity and business savvy. He stated that he was very impressed by the company's strong professional environment and complete lack of nepotism. Harry did express concerns about the winery's new CFO. He felt that Rob was too eager to "make his mark" on the company as evidenced by the implementation of the company's new IS. According to Harry, Rob believed the winery's old IS was limiting CA's future because of its inability to provide accurate data in a timely manner and was insistent that a new system be implemented. Several of the winery's internal memos reviewed by you indicated that Rob was the real force behind the new system.

You asked Harry if there were any disagreements with management about either accounting principles or his firm's audit procedures. He quickly mentioned that his firm had always enjoyed a very good relationship with CA until Rob became CFO. When you asked him to explain further, Harry said that Rob is very knowledgeable, but also more aggressive than CA's former CFO. He specifically mentioned that last year's audit team noted policy changes related to Accounts Receivable and Accounts Payable. With respect to receivables, the company instituted more aggressive collection procedures and reduced the Allowance for Bad Debts by more than $100,000 from the previous year. The company also implemented a practice of paying vendors who offer discounts within that discount period, but simultaneously delayed payments to vendors who offer no discounts by 10 to 15 days beyond the indicated terms. Notwithstanding these changes, Harry said that he was unaware of any significant negative reaction by customers or vendors.

Finally, you asked Harry to explain his understanding of why CA had decided to change audit firms. After a brief silence, he said that Edward and Rob had told him that they believed the company needed a "fresh perspective" and was concerned that his firm would not be able to provide the services required as their company continued its growth.

Financial Statements

Financial statements for the current and preceding two years were provided by Rob Breeden and are included at the end of this narrative. Harry Lawson's firm issued an unqualified audit opinion on the company's financial statements for each of the preceding two years.

REQUIREMENTS

Client acceptance is a challenging process that requires considerable professional judgment. Although such decisions are typically made by highly experienced auditors, you have so impressed the managers and partners in your office that you have been asked to assist with the client acceptance procedures for Chateau Americana.

Before you perform the remaining audit procedures listed on the audit program, identify four to six procedures auditors may perform as part of the client acceptance process. Are any of the procedures identified by you required by generally accepted auditing standards?

Now you are ready to assist the engagement partner, Claire Helton, by completing all open audit procedures on the audit program. Document your work on the provided audit schedules that follow Chateau Americana's financial statements. You should assume that audit schedules CA-104 and CA-105 were properly prepared and have already been included with other relevant audit documentation.

The Winery at Chateau Americana
Audit Program for Client Acceptance

For the Year Ended December 31, 20XX

Reference: _CA-100_
Prepared by: _CH_
Date: _11/14/XX_
Reviewed by: _____

Audit Procedures	Initial	Date	A/S Ref.
1. Obtain an overview of the client's operations by interviewing client personnel and touring the facilities.	_CH_	_11/16/XX_	_CA-104_
2. Obtain permission from the potential client to communicate with the predecessor auditor. Contact the predecessor and request relevant information regarding the client.	_CH_	_11/5/XX_	_CA-105_
3. Brainstorm about and briefly describe financial and non-financial factors that are relevant to the decision to accept the potential client.			_CA-106_
4. Perform preliminary analytical procedures using the financial statements provided by the client. Calculate ratios for comparison to the industry averages provided.			_CA-107_
5. Discuss the overall results of the preliminary analytical procedures. Identify relationships or areas that may be of concern during the audit.			_CA-108_
6. Based on the information obtained do you recommend that the firm accept or not accept the potential client? Briefly explain the basis for your recommendation.			_CA-109_
7. Identify matters that should be included in an engagement letter for this client.			_CA-110_

The Winery at Chateau Americana, Inc.
Balance Sheets as of December 31, 20XX – 20XV
(In Thousands)

ASSETS

	(Unaudited) 20XX	20XW	20XV
CURRENT ASSETS			
Cash	$ 3,005	$ 2,992	$ 3,281
Accounts receivable (net of allowance)	5,241	4,816	3,703
Investments	3,095	2,081	2,294
Production inventories	11,578	10,407	9,107
Finished goods inventories	4,015	3,902	3,567
Prepaid expenses	142	85	69
Total Current Assets	27,076	$ 24,283	$ 22,021
PROPERTY, PLANT & EQUIPMENT	30,230	28,135	27,612
Less accumulated depreciation	15,277	14,096	13,185
Net Property, Plant & Equipment	14,953	14,039	14,427
TOTAL ASSETS	$ 42,029	$ 38,322	$ 36,448

LIABILITIES AND SHAREHOLDERS' EQUITY

	20XX	20XW	20XV
CURRENT LIABILITIES			
Accounts payable	$ 4,988	$ 3,683	$ 2,221
Accrued expenses	599	569	640
Notes payable	813	654	891
Current portion of long term debt	410	525	464
Payroll taxes withheld and payable	100	95	96
Federal income tax payable	172	157	134
Total Current Liabilities	7,082	5,683	4,446
LONG TERM DEBT	7,229	6,918	7,983
TOTAL LIABILITIES	14,311	12,601	12,429
SHAREHOLDERS' EQUITY			
Common stock (No par value, 5,000,000 shares authorized, 45,000 shares issued)	90	90	90
Additional paid-in capital	3,567	3,567	3,567
Retained earnings	24,061	22,064	20,362
Total Shareholders' Equity	27,718	25,721	24,019
TOTAL LIABILITIES AND SHAREHOLDERS' EQUITY	$ 42,029	$ 38,322	$ 36,448

The Winery at Chateau Americana, Inc.
Statements of Income for Years Ended December 31, 20XX – 20XV
(In Thousands)

	(Projected) 20XX	20XW	20XV
Sales	$ 21,945	$ 20,189	$ 18,170
Cost of goods sold	11,543	10,525	9,777
Gross profit	10,402	9,664	8,393
Selling, general and administrative expenses	7,017	6,824	6,218
Operating income	3,386	2,840	2,175
Interest expense	360	211	257
Provision for income taxes	1,028	927	483
Net income	$ 1,997	$ 1,702	$ 1,435

Selected Industry Ratios

	20XX	20XW
Current Ratio	4.9	4.7
Accounts Receivable Turnover	4.42	4.30
Average Days to Collect Accounts Receivable	82.58	84.88
Inventory Turnover	0.67	0.80
Days in Inventory	545	456
Assets to Equity	1.99	2.14
Debt to Equity Ratio	0.99	1.14
Times Interest Earned	6.91	7.29
Return on Assets	5.56 %	7.61 %
Return on Equity	5.92 %	10.76 %

The Winery at Chateau Americana
Evaluation of Financial and Non-financial Factors

For the Year Ended December 31, 20XX

Reference:	*CA-106*
Prepared by:	
Date:	
Reviewed by:	

Financial factors:

Non-financial factors:

The Winery at Chateau Americana
Preliminary Analytical Procedures

Reference: _CA-107_
Prepared by: _____
Date: _____

For the Year Ended December 31, 20XX

Reviewed by: _____

Ratio	Industry Ratios		Chateau Americana	Notes
	20XX	20XW	20XX	
Current Ratio	4.9	4.7		
Accounts Receivable Turnover	4.42	4.30		
Average Days to Collect A/R	82.58	84.88		
Inventory Turnover	0.67	0.80		
Days in Inventory	545	456		
Assets to Equity	1.99	2.14		
Debt to Equity Ratio	0.99	1.14		
Times Interest Earned	6.91	7.29		
Return on Assets	5.56%	7.61%		
Return on Equity	5.92%	10.76%		

The Winery at Chateau Americana
Summary of Preliminary Analytical Procedures

For the Year Ended December 31, 20XX

Reference:	*CA-108*
Prepared by:	
Date:	
Reviewed by:	

The Winery at Chateau Americana
Client Acceptance Recommendation
For the Year Ended December 31, 20XX

Reference: _CA-109_
Prepared by: _____
Date: _____
Reviewed by: _____

Recommendation:

_____ Accept the potential client

_____ Do not accept the potential client

Basis for above recommendation:

The Winery at Chateau Americana
Establishing an Understanding with the Client
For the Year Ended December 31, 20XX

Reference: *CA-110*
Prepared by:
Date:
Reviewed by:

Matters to include in an engagement letter:

Ingraham / Jenkins

UNDERSTANDING THE BUSINESS ENVIRONMENT:
The Winery At Chateau Americana

LEARNING OBJECTIVES

After completing and discussing this case, you should be able to:

- Describe and document information related to the evaluation of a client's business environment
- Describe sources of business risks and understand the relationship between business risk and the risk of material misstatements in the financial statements
- Describe the types of information that should be used in assessing the risk of material misstatements in the financial statements
- Articulate the types of questions that may be used to conduct interviews of client personnel

INTRODUCTION

Chateau Americana (CA) recently hired your accounting firm to perform an audit of its financial statements for the year ended December 31, 20XX. Your partner, Claire Helton, approached you several days ago with a request for help in planning this year's audit engagement. She asked for assistance in three specific areas: understanding the winery's business environment, assessing business risks, and identifying and assessing factors relevant to the risk of material misstatements in CA's financial statements. As you work to develop an understanding of the business environment, Claire asked that you specifically consider factors related to business operations, management and corporate governance, business objectives and strategies, and performance measurement.

Claire invited you to accompany her on a recent visit to the winery during which she interviewed CA's president Edward Summerfield, vice-president of marketing Taylor Summerfield, chief financial officer Rob Breeden, and the vice-president of winery operations Jacques Dupuis. The following transcripts were taken from those interviews. At the end of the transcripts, you will also find excerpts from various trade publications which will help you learn more about the wine industry.

INTERVIEW TRANSCRIPTS

Claire: Edward, thank you for meeting with us today. We're here to learn more about the winery's history and your vision of the company's future.

Edward: Well Claire, we're thrilled to have you and the rest of your team working with us. I believe Chateau Americana has an amazing future. Many fine people have worked hard to make this company great and we've endured our share of bumps along the way, but I think most of us would agree that we've learned a great deal over the years and have a stronger company as a consequence.

Let me give you a bit of background about us. After spending more than 20 years working for other companies in the wine industry, I decided to start my own company. Although my family was a bit skeptical at first, they were and continue to be supportive. The winery has become the typical family business with a good deal of family involvement. My daughter is vice president of marketing, my son-in-law is vice president of winery operations, and several of my grandchildren have worked for us during their summer breaks. In all, we have approximately 250 permanent employees and we hire an additional 30 to 40 seasonal employees for harvest. Many of our employees have been with us for a number of years and we have been fortunate to have very little employee turnover.

Our current production is approximately 385,000 cases with capacity for an additional 80,000 cases. Our intention is to grow our business to a sustained level between 410,000 and 450,000 cases. We expect to achieve this level within the next three to five years. Our wines are sold in more than 20 states and we have exclusive distribution agreements with several small wine distributors in a few states. We have a sales force of highly motivated and experienced individuals. We plan to add several new sales positions in the coming months.

The wine business is highly competitive and because we're one of almost 1,800 wineries, we have to remain vigilant if we want to continue to thrive. Our geographic location assists us in staying abreast of industry trends. Almost half of all domestic wineries are in California, so there's a concentration of talent here that's nowhere else in the U.S.

Claire: I've read about the trend toward consolidation in the industry. How will this trend affect your company?

Edward: Well, that's a great question. As I mentioned a minute ago, this is a family business and we have no interest in being taken over by a bigger winery. My family and I have had a number of discussions about this and we all agree that this company is our family's future.

I'm certain that we will need to be vigilant as we move forward, and I believe that our people are committed to being as efficient and innovative as possible while maintaining our winery's commitment to its small business values.

Claire: What kinds of innovations have been made recently?

Edward: We have adopted new technologies in our winemaking process and even more recently in our accounting information system. I understand that you plan to talk with Rob later today. I would suggest you speak to him about the details.

However, I can give you my perspective on our new accounting information system. When we first started our company, we were very small and primarily relied on a paper trail to document our business. We had numerous journals and ledgers and were constantly relying on information that was outdated. Over the last ten years, we've become much more reliant on technology and until about 18 months ago we were using a combination of software programs to maintain our records. I became convinced several years ago that we needed to move to a more integrated system that would grow with us and provide more current information. Rob was instrumental in helping us make the transition to the new system.

Claire: How have your employees reacted to the new information system? Have you had any turnover related to the system change?

Edward: Like any change, some employees have been unhappy with the new system, but they'll become accustomed to it. We've had some turnover in accounting, but I don't know the details. You'll have to ask Rob about that.

Claire: Okay, I have questions on two additional matters before we meet with Rob. First, how would you describe the management group's operating style and philosophy? Second, could you describe how the board of directors functions?

Edward: Well, as I've mentioned before, this is a family company. All of us place a great deal of value on integrity and hard work. I, along with the rest of management, support open communications and encourage employees to approach any member of management with suggestions and concerns. Since we started our business in 1980, we have been focused on producing excellent wines and establishing a solid reputation. I believe that we've stayed true to our mission and I feel strongly that we have employees that are committed to the same values.

Our board of directors is comprised of three employees and four non-employees. I serve as chairman of the board. The other employee board members are my daughter Taylor and Rob Breeden, our CFO. The four non-employee board members are my wife Charlotte, Bill Jameson, and Susan Martinez, and Terrence Dillard. Bill and Susan are local business owners and have a great deal of experience with family-owned businesses. Terrence is an attorney with whom I have a longstanding personal relationship. Like me, my wife worked in the wine industry before we started Chateau Americana. I wanted our company to benefit from her work experience, so she agreed to serve on our board.

Claire: How often does the board meet and generally how long are the meetings?

Edward: The length of the meetings varies quite a bit, but a typical meeting lasts for two to three hours. We generally meet four times a year, but we can meet as often as our operations necessitate.

Claire: Do you have either an audit committee or a compensation committee?

Edward: No. Our company is so small that no one on the board has ever felt it necessary to establish such committees. Everyone is on the same page regarding our company and its future, so we always discuss and resolve any differences that may arise during our meetings.

Claire: Those are all of my questions for now. Thanks very much for taking the time to meet with us. We'll let you know if we have other questions.

◆◆

After meeting with Edward, you met with Taylor Summerfield, the company's vice president of marketing.

Claire: Taylor, it's great to see you again. We wanted to meet with you so we could learn about the winery's marketing strategy and how the company is positioning itself in the industry.

Taylor: The wine industry is very competitive. Most consumers choose wine based on just three factors: price, brand, or variety. In addition, consumers tend to buy wines only for special occasions. Domestic consumers have a long way to go before they purchase and consume wines in the same patterns as Europeans.

In the past, we've relied on a product differentiation strategy. That is, we have not competed on price, but have focused our energies and resources on appealing to a certain set of wine drinkers. For instance, several of our wines have won highly coveted awards which we have tried to leverage into targeted advertising campaigns aimed at consumers who are willing to spend $10 to $30 for a good bottle of wine. We've found that many of these consumers are baby boomers.

Claire: How are other demographic groups addressed by your marketing strategy?

Taylor: Although baby boomers purchase a significant percentage of our wines, we are making inroads with younger consumers. There are a significant number of individuals between the ages of 35 and 64 who have sufficient disposable income and the desire to purchase better table wines. We are currently discussing some new strategies targeted at that segment of the population. We have discussed the possibility of sponsoring or co-sponsoring certain events such as arts festivals, golf tournaments, and various charity functions.

Claire: What is your advertising budget?

Taylor: Approximately $750,000.

Claire: Is this sufficient?

Taylor: I would like to devote more of our resources to advertising and marketing, but I'm also aware of some of our other needs. My father and I meet frequently about the company's marketing strategy and we both agree that we need to increase the advertising budget. I expect that we will increase our budget by 10 to 20 percent in the next couple of years.

Claire: Turning to your customer base, do you have any *key* customers?

Taylor: We've specifically tried to avoid over reliance on a single customer or a small number of customers. However, we have developed close relationships with several reasonably large distributors. We monitor sales and collections activity with these customers to limit our exposure. I should tell you that no single customer accounts for more than five percent of our annual sales.

Claire: One last question if I may. How large is your sales force?

Taylor: Currently, we have 20 sales people. We intend to add several sales positions in the near future to help with our projected sales growth. Our goal is to increase sales by eight to ten percent per year.

Claire: Is that a realistic goal?

Taylor: I think so. Our sales growth has averaged approximately nine percent over the last several years. I feel confident that a bigger sales force will allow us to easily increase our sales.

Claire: Great, thanks for meeting with us. We'll be in touch if we have any other questions.

♦ ♦

Following the meeting with Taylor, you made your way to Rob Breeden's office. Rob is the company's chief financial officer.

Claire: Rob, thank you for meeting with us this afternoon. We wanted to talk about several issues. Let's start with the company's accounting department. Can you describe the personnel and the general operations of the department?

Rob: Sure, we have a great group of folks in accounting. With the exception of two individuals who left within the last several months we've had very little turnover. We only use full-time employees in the department. Each employee reports directly to me and has very clearly defined responsibilities.

Edward is very concerned about employee training and so everyone is encouraged to maintain their education. In fact, the company reimburses employees for the cost of courses taken at the local university. We've been very pleased at the employee response to the policy. I believe it helps us retain our people.

Claire: Next, can you tell us about the new accounting information system. Can you give us a brief overview of the system and explain why you chose it?

Rob: The system is the result of an intense in-house development process. During my tenure with my former employer we developed a similar system using database technology. Here we based our system on Access. The software is really quite powerful and it allowed us to develop all of the modules that we need to have updated and accurate information.

In addition, the new system will easily accommodate our needs for the foreseeable future. Integration was also important to us as our previous system was not well integrated. With this system, all of our functional areas are linked so that employees have access to the same updated information. The integration has dramatically improved our operations in areas such as purchasing, shipping, and cash management.

Claire: I understand there has been some employee turnover as a consequence of frustrations with the new system.

Rob: We've had a few employees to leave in recent months, but I'm not sure that I would agree with the contention that they left because of frustration with the system. We have made every effort to train our people and to address their concerns, but I recognize that some individuals may still not be happy with changes that I've made.

Claire: You mentioned cash management – I noticed the company generally maintains a healthy cash balance.

Rob: Yes, we've really improved our cash management in the last 12 to 18 months. There are several reasons for the improvement. First, we've instituted a new disbursements policy that allows us to take advantage of any early payment discounts. This policy alone has saved us quite a bit of money. We continually monitor our cash collections and credit granting practices to avoid excessive write-offs. In fact, one of my concerns when I started working with the winery was the company's potential exposure to several large customers. Since my arrival, we've dramatically cut our reliance on certain customers. Finally, our new AIS has enabled us to monitor our cash position more closely than ever before.

Claire: So, I take it that you're comfortable with the reliability of the financial reports that are generated?

Rob: Absolutely. I was less comfortable with the old system because of the lack of integration. In addition, I've encouraged Edward and the Board to be more active in reviewing our monthly financials. My sense is that they were less involved in the financial aspect of the business prior to my arrival because of their relationship with the former CFO.

Claire: Have they become more involved?

Rob: Yes, Edward and I meet regularly to review the financial statements and I make a presentation to the board at every meeting.

Claire: How is the company financed?

Rob: Like many similar companies, the winery is financed through a combination of the owners' personal wealth and debt. The Summerfield family invested in the company many years ago and they have been rewarded handsomely. The company does have a modest amount of long-term debt, but we are reducing that debt as our operations allow. We plan to eliminate most of the outstanding long-term debt within the next three to five years.

Claire: Does the company have ready access to a line of credit?

Rob: Yes. Edward has developed very strong relationships with several local banks. We currently have a line of credit at Bank of Huntington.

Claire: With respect to the company's equity - are there any non-family stockholders?

Rob: No. Although we've discussed plans about a future IPO, Edward and the family have been reluctant to issue shares to anyone outside of the family. Their view is that non-family ownership may complicate operations in an unnecessary way.

Claire: Do you agree with them?

Rob: Yes. I don't see any value in diluting the family's ownership of the company given our current financial position.

Claire: Are there any related party transactions?

Rob: None to speak of really. Edward personally owns some of the equipment that we use in the winery, but there are no other significant transactions. We pay him approximately $9,000 each month.

Claire: Okay, we'll need to get a copy of that lease agreement. Let's move on to compensation matters. Give us an overview of the company's compensation philosophy.

Rob: Edward is a self-made man. He expects employees to work hard and believes the company should pay them well. Given our status as a family-owned business, employees are viewed as more than labor.

Claire: Are there any incentive compensation plans?

Rob: Our salespeople are paid a base salary plus a commission. All other employees receive annual bonuses based on the company's overall performance.

Claire: Does management participate in this annual bonus plan?

Rob: Yes. Everyone has the potential to receive a bonus.

Claire: What is the typical bonus?

Rob: The average bonus is approximately 10 percent of an employee's annual salary, but we've had bonuses as high as 30 percent.

Claire: What basis is used to calculate the bonuses?

Rob: Our bonus plan emphasizes operating efficiency and effectiveness. We consider factors such as employee performance evaluations, production efficiencies and innovations, sales, and profits.

Claire: So, you would say that there is a strong link between performance and compensation.

Rob: Yes, this is not a company that tolerates lazy employees or lackluster performance.

Claire: I'm certain it's not. You have been really helpful this afternoon. Thank you for your time Rob.

◆◆

Your final meeting of the day was with Jacques Dupuis, vice-president of winery operations.

Claire: Good afternoon Jacques. We appreciate your time this afternoon. We have just a few questions for you. How would you characterize the winery's manufacturing facilities?

Jacques: Absolutely. The winery has world-class manufacturing facilities. Edward has built a company that nicely blends the best of traditional winemaking with modern technology. I have no doubt that we have the equipment, experience and capacity to produce world-class wines.

Claire: What is the winery's average current production? Do you have any concerns about meeting production goals?

Jacques: We typically produce 380,000 to 390,000 cases of wine per year. We are close to capacity. I would estimate that we could produce an additional 20,000 to 30,000 cases without sacrificing quality. So long as our goals don't surpass 420,000 cases we have adequate production capacity.

Claire: Are there plans to increase production capacity?

Jacques: I don't believe so.

Claire: Alright. Do you have an adequate work force to manage production needs?

Jacques: Generally we are able to hire as many workers as necessary. However, we have had some difficulties in finding good, solid workers recently. It's as if people just don't want to work hard anymore.

Claire: I understand. You've been very helpful this afternoon. Thank you for your time. We may want to speak with you again if you don't mind.

Jacques: I'm glad to help. Just let me know if you have other questions.

◆◆

You returned to the office following your meeting with Rob to find that Claire had asked one of the firm's assistants to gather information to help in your understanding of the wine industry. The assistant prepared the following summary observations based on her readings of various trade publications.

- The wine industry spent slightly more than $100 million on marketing activities in the U.S. in 20XU.

- U.S. wine consumers are more brand-oriented than consumers in other countries.

- There has been an increase in non-traditional wine marketing including direct mail, offbeat advertising and such Internet sites as Wine.com.

- The U.S. wine market is characterized by a large number of wineries producing a wide variety of products, most with a small market share.

- In the fragmented wine market, the middle tier of medium-sized wine producers is expected to fall prey to merger and acquisition activity over the next few years. Smaller niche producers will need to specialize if they are to survive.

- Supermarkets dominate off-premises sales of wine. Their distribution strategy focuses on improved merchandising, stocking larger bottle sizes and strong price promotions.

- Significant demand for wines during the late 1990s led to rising prices, resulting in faster growth in sales value than in sales volume.

- Wine consumption is directly related to income. High income families are much more likely to consume wine than lower income families.

- Prosperous baby boomers are expected to increase their wine consumption in the future, especially of premium wines.

- The trend towards consolidation is expected to continue as companies search for strategies to benefit from economies of scale in production and distribution.

REQUIREMENTS

Claire Helton, the partner in charge of the Chateau Americana audit engagement, has asked that you complete select audit procedures relevant to understanding the company's business environment. Document your work on the audit schedules that follow the audit program.

The Winery at Chateau Americana	Reference:	_UB-200_
Audit Program for Understanding	Prepared by:	
the Business Environment	Date:	
For the Year Ended December 31, 20XX	Reviewed by:	

Audit Procedures	Initial	Date	A/S Ref.
1. Document your assessment of Chateau Americana on each of the following criteria: a. industry, regulatory and other external factors, b. nature of the entity, c. objectives and strategies, d. measurement and review of the entity's financial performance.			_UB-201_
2. Document your assessment of Chateau Americana's control environment.			_UB-202_ _UB-203_
3. Identify and discuss factors affecting Chateau Americana's business risk. For each of the factors, indicate the client's business objective that is put at risk.			_UB-204_
4. Based on your knowledge of Chateau Americana, what accounts are likely to have a lower risk of material misstatement and what accounts are likely to have higher risk of material misstatement? Briefly describe the basis for each account's assessment.			_UB-205_

The Winery at Chateau Americana
Evaluation of the Entity and its Environment

For the Year Ended December 31, 20XX

Reference: _UB-201_
Prepared by:
Date:
Reviewed by:

Industry, regulatory and other external factors:

Nature of the entity:

Objectives and strategies:

Measurement and review of the entity's financial performance:

The Winery at Chateau Americana
Assessment of Control Environment

Reference: *UB-202*
Prepared by: _____
Date: _____

For the Year Ended December 31, 20XX

Reviewed by: _____

Communication and enforcement of integrity and ethical values:

Commitment to competence:

Participation of those charged with governance:

Management's philosophy and operating style:

The Winery at Chateau Americana
Assessment of Control Environment

For the Year Ended December 31, 20XX

Reference: _UB-203_

Prepared by: _____

Date: _____

Reviewed by: _____

Organizational structure:

Assignment of authority and responsibility:

Human resource policies and practices:

Overall Assessment: Summarize your overall assessment of Chateau Americana's control environment by selecting from among the following statements:

_____ The overall control environment is weak.
_____ The overall control environment is moderately weak.
_____ The overall control environment is neither weak nor strong.
_____ The overall control environment is moderately strong.
_____ The overall control environment is strong.

The Winery at Chateau Americana
Business Risks and At-risk Objectives

For the Year Ended December 31, 20XX

Reference: _UB-204_
Prepared by: _____
Date: _____
Reviewed by: _____

Factors affecting business risks:

Business objectives that are put at risk:

Ingraham / Jenkins

The Winery at Chateau Americana
Evaluation of Potential Misstatements

For the Year Ended December 31, 20XX

Accounts likely to have a lower risk of material misstatement:

Accounts like to have a higher risk of material misstatement:

IDENTIFICATION OF AUDIT TESTS FOR THE EXPENDITURE CYCLE (ACQUISITIONS AND CASH DISBURSEMENTS): The Winery at Chateau Americana

LEARNING OBJECTIVES

After completing and discussing this case, you should be able to:

- Recognize common business documents used with purchases and cash disbursements
- Recognize common control activities used to process purchases and cash disbursements
- Identify control activities that reduce the likelihood of material misstatements and link the activities to management assertions
- Design tests of controls for control activities related to purchases and cash disbursements
- Design substantive tests of transactions to detect material misstatements for non-payroll accounts in the expenditure cycle
- Design analytical tests to detect potential material misstatements for non-payroll accounts in the expenditure cycle
- Design substantive tests of balances to detect material misstatements for accounts payable
- Link tests of controls and substantive tests to management assertions related to purchases, cash payments, and accounts payable
- Identify significant deficiencies and material weaknesses for non-payroll expenditure cycle accounts

INTRODUCTION

Chateau Americana (CA) has an annual production of approximately 385,000 cases of wine. Production of the 385,000 cases of wine requires roughly 3,200 tons of grapes. One-fourth of the needed grapes are harvested from CA's 125-acre vineyard, the remaining grapes are predominantly purchased from California vineyards. Other purchases associated with the production of wine include oak barrels, bottles, cork, neck wrappers, and labels. CA also has non-payroll administrative, marketing, and maintenance expenditures associated with its wine operations. Marketing expenditures such as priority distribution, special promotions, and print advertising have substantially increased in the past year to improve CA's market penetration.

BACKGROUND INFORMATION ABOUT THE AUDIT

CA has the following general ledger accounts related to purchasing and cash disbursement activities:

- Inventory – Production
- Prepaid Expenses
- Accounts Payable
- Accrued Expenses
- Cost of Goods Sold
- Occupancy Expense
- Marketing Expense
- Communications Expense
- Professional Services Expense
- Supplies Expense
- Data Processing Expense
- Travel and Entertainment Expense
- Insurance Expense
- Dues and Subscriptions Expense
- Tax Expense
- Maintenance Expense
- Automobile Expense
- Lease Expense
- Other Operating Expense
- Miscellaneous Expense

In accordance with professional standards, Mikel Frucella, audit manager, reviewed CA's control environment, risk assessment policies, and monitoring system and has assessed them as strong. Julia Granger, staff auditor, reviewed CA's information system and control activities related to purchases and cash disbursements and prepared the enclosed flowcharts (referenced in the top right hand corner as *E-110, E-111,* and *E-112*). Mikel has decided there is no need to document the company's policies nor perform tests of controls for purchase returns and allowances as the number and size of purchase returns and allowances is relatively small.

As the audit senior, you have been assigned responsibility for (1) identifying internal control activities that assure that non-payroll purchase and cash disbursement transactions are properly stated in all material respects, (2) developing tests of controls that test the design and operating effectiveness of identified internal control activities, and (3) identifying substantive tests to detect material misstatements related to non-payroll expenditure cycle accounts. You have conducted some preliminary discussions with client personnel and noted the following

- Purchase returns and allowances transactions are recorded in the purchases journal
- Purchase discounts are recorded in the cash disbursements journal
- Adjustments to expenditure cycle accounts are recorded in the general journal and require preparation of a prenumbered adjustment memo

REQUIREMENTS

Complete steps 5 through 8 in the Expenditure Cycle Planning Audit Program (audit schedule *E-100*) and document your work on audit schedules *E-100, E-120, E-121, E-130, E-140, E-141, E-150, E-151, E-160, E-161, E-170,* and *E-171*. Julia Granger has already completed steps 1 through 4 and has documented the results of her work on audit schedules *E-100, E-110, E-111,* and *E-112*. Assume that the client performs the control activities identified in the flowcharts.

The Winery at Chateau Americana
Expenditure Cycle Planning Audit Program

Reference: _E-100_
Prepared by: _JG_
Date: _11/12/XX_

For the Year Ended: December 31, 20XX

Reviewed by: _____

Audit Procedures	Initial	Date	A/S Ref.
1. Obtain and study a copy of the client's policies and procedures manuals related to purchases and cash disbursements.	JG	11/12/XX	N/A
2. Discuss with and observe client personnel performing control activities related to purchases and cash disbursements.	JG	11/12/XX	N/A
3. Perform a walk-through of the client's polices and procedures related to purchases and cash disbursements.	JG	11/12/XX	N/A
4. Obtain or prepare a flowchart for purchases and cash disbursements showing control activities, document flows, and records.	JG	11/12/XX	E-110 E-111 E-112
5. Document client control activities that reduce the likelihood of material misstatements for management assertions related to purchases and cash disbursements.			E-120 E-121
6. Document potential internal control deficiencies.			E-130
7. Use the planning audit test matrices to list potential tests of controls related to purchases and cash disbursements.			E-140 E-141
8. Use the planning audit test matrices to identify potential			
a. Substantive tests of transactions,			E-150 E-151
b. Analytical tests, and			E-160 E-161
c. Tests of balances related to non-payroll expenditure cycle accounts.			E-170 E-171

The Winery at Chateau Americana
Expenditure Cycle - Purchases Flowchart

For the Year Ended December 31, 20XX

Reference:	*E-110*
Prepared by:	*Client/JG*
Date:	*11/12/XX*
Reviewed by:	

Purchasing

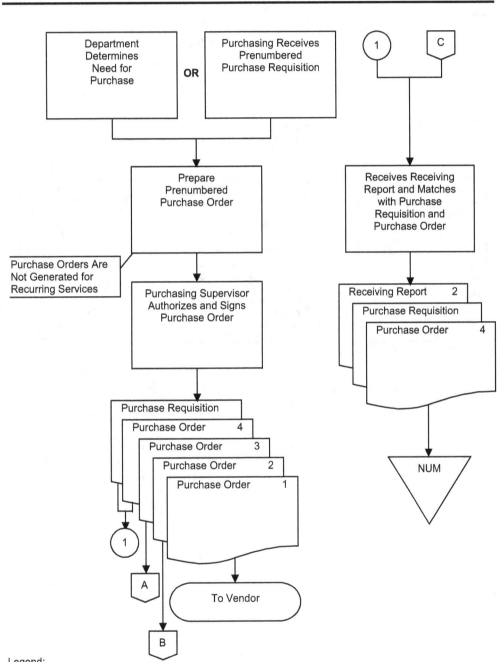

Legend:
NUM - filed numerically by Purchase Order number
A - off-page connector
B - off-page connector
C - off-page connector

The Winery at Chateau Americana
Expenditure Cycle - Purchases Flowchart

For the Year Ended December 31, 20XX

Reference: *E-111*
Prepared by: *Client/JG*
Date: *11/12/XX*
Reviewed by: _____

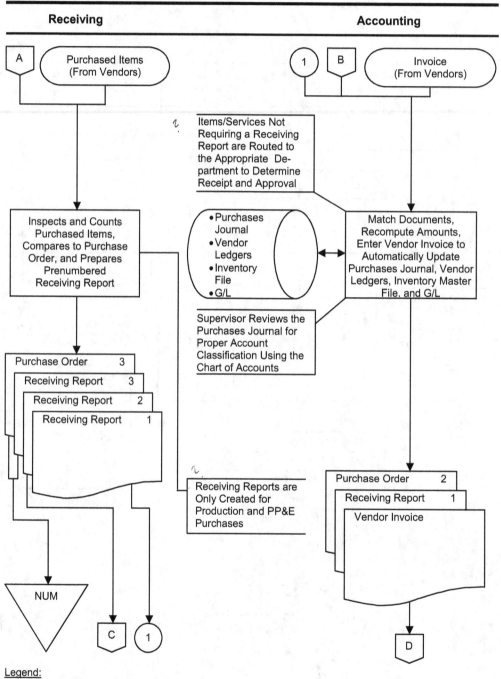

Receiving	Accounting

A — Purchased Items (From Vendors)

1 | B — Invoice (From Vendors)

Items/Services Not Requiring a Receiving Report are Routed to the Appropriate Department to Determine Receipt and Approval

Inspects and Counts Purchased Items, Compares to Purchase Order, and Prepares Prenumbered Receiving Report

- Purchases Journal
- Vendor Ledgers
- Inventory File
- G/L

Match Documents, Recompute Amounts, Enter Vendor Invoice to Automatically Update Purchases Journal, Vendor Ledgers, Inventory Master File, and G/L

Supervisor Reviews the Purchases Journal for Proper Account Classification Using the Chart of Accounts

Purchase Order 3
Receiving Report 3
Receiving Report 2
Receiving Report 1

Receiving Reports are Only Created for Production and PP&E Purchases

Purchase Order 2
Receiving Report 1
Vendor Invoice

NUM

C

1

D

Legend:
NUM - filed numerically by Receiving Report number
A - off-page connector
B - off-page connector
C - off-page connector
D - off-page connector

The Winery at Chateau Americana
Expenditure Cycle - Cash Disbursement Flowchart

For the Year Ended December 31, 20XX

Reference:	*E-112*
Prepared by:	*Client/JG*
Date:	*11/12/XX*
Reviewed by:	

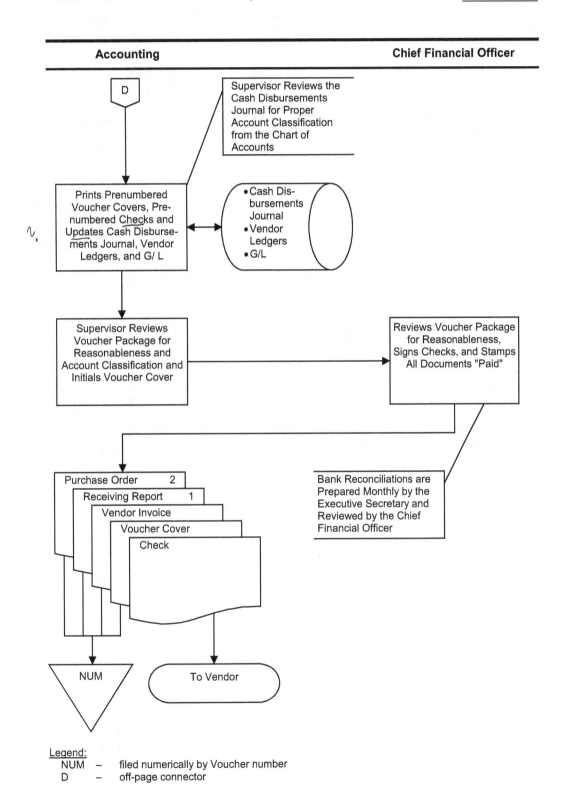

Accounting   **Chief Financial Officer**

D

Supervisor Reviews the Cash Disbursements Journal for Proper Account Classification from the Chart of Accounts

Prints Prenumbered Voucher Covers, Pre-numbered Checks and Updates Cash Disburse-ments Journal, Vendor Ledgers, and G/ L

- Cash Dis-bursements Journal
- Vendor Ledgers
- G/L

Supervisor Reviews Voucher Package for Reasonableness and Account Classification and Initials Voucher Cover

Reviews Voucher Package for Reasonableness, Signs Checks, and Stamps All Documents "Paid"

Bank Reconciliations are Prepared Monthly by the Executive Secretary and Reviewed by the Chief Financial Officer

Purchase Order   2
Receiving Report   1
Vendor Invoice
Voucher Cover
Check

NUM

To Vendor

Legend:
NUM – filed numerically by Voucher number
D – off-page connector

The Winery at Chateau Americana
Expenditure Cycle – Purchases Control Activities
    Matrix
For the Year Ended December 31, 20XX

Reference: *E-120*
Prepared by:
Date:
Reviewed by:

Control Activities	Existence	Rights and Obligations	Valuation	Presentation and Disclosure	Completeness
1) Purchasing supervisor reviews and signs all purchase orders.	X	X			
Identify the management assertion(s) each control activity affects with an "X."					

The Winery at Chateau Americana
Expenditure Cycle – Cash Disbursements Control
   Activities Matrix
For the Year Ended December 31, 20XX

Reference: *E-121*
Prepared by: _____
Date: _____
Reviewed by: _____

Control Activities	Existence	Rights and Obligations	Valuation	Presentation and Disclosure	Completeness
Identify the management assertion(s) each control activity affects with an "X."					

Ingraham / Jenkins

The Winery at Chateau Americana
Expenditure Cycle – Internal Control Deficiencies

For the Year Ended December 31, 20XX

Reference: *E-130*
Prepared by:
Date:
Reviewed by:

Internal Control Deficiencies	Client Personnel Discussed With	SD	MW
1) *The client does not internally account for all used receiving reports.*		*Yes*	*No*

Legend:
SD – Significant Deficiency (Yes or No)
MW – Material Weakness (Yes or No)

The Winery at Chateau Americana
Expenditure Cycle - Tests of Controls Planning Matrix

For the Year Ended December 31, 20XX

Reference: *E-140*
Prepared by: _____
Date: _____
Reviewed by: _____

Tests of Controls	Purchases					Cash Disbursements					Accounts Payable				
	Existence	Rights/Obligations	Valuation	Presentation/Disclosure	Completeness	Existence	Rights/Obligations	Valuation	Presentation/Disclosure	Completeness	Existence	Rights/Obligations	Valuation	Presentation/Disclosure	Completeness
TC1) Inquire and observe the purchasing supervisor reviewing and signing purchase orders.	W										W	W			

Indicate whether the test provides Strong (S), Moderate (M), or Weak (W) evidence for the specific management assertion.

The Winery at Chateau Americana
Expenditure Cycle - Tests of Controls Planning Matrix

For the Year Ended December 31, 20XX

Reference: *E-141*
Prepared by:
Date:
Reviewed by:

Tests of Controls	Purchases					Cash Disbursements					Accounts Payable				
	Existence	Rights/Obligations	Valuation	Presentation/Disclosure	Completeness	Existence	Rights/Obligations	Valuation	Presentation/Disclosure	Completeness	Existence	Rights/Obligations	Valuation	Presentation/Disclosure	Completeness

Indicate whether the test provides Strong (S), Moderate (M), or Weak (W) evidence for the specific management assertion.

The Winery at Chateau Americana
Expenditure Cycle - Substantive Tests of Transactions
Planning Matrix
For the Year Ended December 31, 20XX

Reference: *E-150*
Prepared by:
Date:
Reviewed by:

Substantive Tests of Transactions	Purchases					Cash Disbursements					Accounts Payable				
	Existence	Rights/Obligations	Valuation	Presentation/Disclosure	Completeness	Existence	Rights/Obligations	Valuation	Presentation/Disclosure	Completeness	Existence	Rights/Obligations	Valuation	Presentation/Disclosure	Completeness
TT1) Vouch purchase transactions recorded in the purchases journal to supporting documents.	M		M	M							M		M	M	

Indicate whether the test provides Strong (S), Moderate (M), or Weak (W) evidence for the specific management assertion.

The Winery at Chateau Americana
Expenditure Cycle - Substantive Tests of Transactions
   Planning Matrix
For the Year Ended December 31, 20XX

Reference: *E-151*
Prepared by: _____
Date: _____
Reviewed by: _____

Substantive Tests of Transactions	Purchases					Cash Disbursements					Accounts Payable				
	Existence	Rights/Obligations	Valuation	Presentation/Disclosure	Completeness	Existence	Rights/Obligations	Valuation	Presentation/Disclosure	Completeness	Existence	Rights/Obligations	Valuation	Presentation/Disclosure	Completeness

Indicate whether the test provides Strong (S), Moderate (M), or Weak (W) evidence for the specific management assertion.

The Winery at Chateau Americana
Expenditure Cycle – Analytical Tests Planning Matrix

Reference: *E-160*
Prepared by: _____
Date: _____

For the Year Ended December 31, 20XX

Reviewed by: _____

Analytical Tests	Purchases					Cash Disbursements					Accounts Payable				
	Existence	Rights/Obligations	Valuation	Presentation/Disclosure	Completeness	Existence	Rights/Obligations	Valuation	Presentation/Disclosure	Completeness	Existence	Rights/Obligations	Valuation	Presentation/Disclosure	Completeness
AT1) Scan the year-end vendor ledgers for large, unusual, related party or debit balances and perform follow-up procedures for each one identified.	M		M	M				M	M	M	M	M	M		M

Indicate whether the test provides Strong (S), Moderate (M), or Weak (W) evidence for the specific management assertion.

The Winery at Chateau Americana
Expenditure Cycle - Analytical Tests Planning Matrix

Reference: _E-161_
Prepared by: _____
Date: _____

For the Year Ended December 31, 20XX

Reviewed by: _____

Analytical Tests	Purchases					Cash Disbursements					Accounts Payable				
	Existence	Rights/Obligations	Valuation	Presentation/Disclosure	Completeness	Existence	Rights/Obligations	Valuation	Presentation/Disclosure	Completeness	Existence	Rights/Obligations	Valuation	Presentation/Disclosure	Completeness

Indicate whether the test provides Strong (S), Moderate (M), or Weak (W) evidence for the specific management assertion.

The Winery at Chateau Americana
Expenditure Cycle - Tests of Balances Planning Matrix

Reference: *E-170*
Prepared by:
Date:
Reviewed by:

For the Year Ended December 31, 20XX

Tests of Balances	Purchases					Cash Disbursements					Accounts Payable				
	Existence	Rights/Obligations	Valuation	Presentation/Disclosure	Completeness	Existence	Rights/Obligations	Valuation	Presentation/Disclosure	Completeness	Existence	Rights/Obligations	Valuation	Presentation/Disclosure	Completeness
TB1) Obtain the last five receiving reports issued before year-end and determine if they were properly included in the purchases journal and year-end vendor ledgers.			W		M								W		M

Indicate whether the test provides Strong (S), Moderate (M), or Weak (W) evidence for the specific management assertion.

The Winery at Chateau Americana
Expenditure Cycle - Tests of Balances Planning Matrix

For the Year Ended December 31, 20XX

Reference: *E-171*
Prepared by:
Date:
Reviewed by:

Tests of Balances	Purchases					Cash Disbursements					Accounts Payable				
	Existence	Rights/Obligations	Valuation	Presentation/Disclosure	Completeness	Existence	Rights/Obligations	Valuation	Presentation/Disclosure	Completeness	Existence	Rights/Obligations	Valuation	Presentation/Disclosure	Completeness

Indicate whether the test provides Strong (S), Moderate (M), or Weak (W) evidence for the specific management assertion.

SELECTION OF AUDIT TESTS AND RISK ASSESSMENT FOR THE EXPENDITURE CYCLE (ACQUISITIONS AND CASH DISBURSEMENTS):
The Winery at Chateau Americana

LEARNING OBJECTIVES

After completing and discussing this case, you should be able to:

- Select appropriate planned tests of controls, substantive tests of transactions, analytical tests, and tests of balances for non-payroll expenditure cycle accounts
- Assess planned control risk for the non-payroll expenditure cycle based on planned tests of controls
- Assess planned detection risk for the non-payroll expenditure cycle based on planned substantive tests

INTRODUCTION

Chateau Americana (CA) has an annual production of approximately 385,000 cases of wine. Production of the 385,000 cases of wine requires roughly 3,200 tons of grapes. One-fourth of the needed grapes are harvested from CA's 125-acre vineyard, the remaining grapes are predominantly purchased from California vineyards. Other purchases associated with the production of wine include oak barrels, bottles, cork, neck wrappers, and labels. CA also has non-payroll administrative, marketing, and maintenance expenditures associated with its wine operations. Marketing expenditures such as priority distribution, special promotions, and print advertising have substantially increased in the past year to improve CA's market penetration.

BACKGROUND INFORMATION ABOUT THE AUDIT

CA has the following general ledger accounts related to purchasing and cash disbursement activities:

- Inventory – Production
- Prepaid Expenses
- Accounts Payable
- Accrued Expenses

- Travel and Entertainment Expense
- Insurance Expense
- Dues and Subscriptions Expense

- Cost of Goods Sold
- Occupancy Expense
- Marketing Expense
- Communications Expense
- Professional Services Expense
- Supplies Expense
- Data Processing Expense

- Tax Expense
- Maintenance Expense
- Automobile Expense
- Lease Expense
- Other Operating Expense
- Miscellaneous Expense

In accordance with professional standards, Mikel Frucella, audit manager, reviewed CA's control environment, risk assessment policies, and monitoring system and has assessed them as strong. Additionally, Mikel determined that tolerable misstatement should be $40,000 for the non-payroll expenditure cycle and that acceptable audit risk should be low. Julia Granger, staff auditor, assessed inherent risk related to purchases, non-payroll cash payments, and accounts payable and prepared the enclosed audit risk matrix (referenced in the top right hand corner as *E-180* and *E-181*). As the audit senior, you have been assigned responsibility for selecting audit procedures to perform for the expenditure cycle that will achieve the desired acceptable audit risk at the lowest possible cost.

REQUIREMENTS

This assignment cannot be completed until the previous CA audit planning assignment is completed. Review the materials in the previous assignment plus the materials in this assignment. Complete audit steps 3 and 4 in the Expenditure Cycle Planning Audit Program – Risk Assessment and Selection of Audit Tests (audit schedule *E-101*) and document your work in audit schedules *E-101, E-140, E-141, E-150, E-151, E-160, E-161, E-170, E-171, E-180, E-182,* and *E-183*. Julia Granger has already completed steps 1 and 2 and has documented the results of her work in audit schedules *E-101, E-180,* and *E-181*.

The Winery at Chateau Americana
Expenditure Cycle Planning Audit Program –
    Risk Assessment and Selection of Audit Tests
Year Ended: December 31, 20XX

Reference:	E-101
Prepared by:	JG
Date:	11/13/XX
Reviewed by:	

Audit Procedures	Initial	Date	A/S Ref.
1. Complete the acceptable audit risk section of the expenditure cycle "Planning Audit Risk Matrix" by obtaining the acceptable audit risk from the general planning audit schedules.	JG	11/13/XX	E-180
2. Form an initial assessment of inherent risk related to non-payroll expenditure cycle accounts and complete the initial inherent risk assessment section of the "Planning Audit Risk Matrix."	JG	11/13/XX	E-180 E-181
3. Select audit tests to perform by circling the procedure number on the audit tests planning matrices (note: audit tests should be selected such that the combination of inherent risk, control risk, and detection risk for each management assertion related to non-payroll expenditure cycle accounts is reduced to the appropriate level).			E-140 E-141 E-150 E-151 E-160 E-161 E-170 E-171
4. Based on the procedures selected in audit step 3, complete the planned control risk and detection risk sections of the expenditure cycle "Planning Audit Risk Matrix."			E-180 E-182 E-183

The Winery at Chateau Americana
Expenditure Cycle - Planning Audit Risk Matrix
For the Year Ended December 31, 20XX

Reference: *E-180*
Prepared by: *JG*
Date: *11/13/XX*
Reviewed by: _____

Tolerable Misstatement: *$40,000, G6*	Reference	Existence*	Rights /Obligations	Valuation	Presentation/Disclosure	Completeness**
Acceptable Audit Risk	G-10	L	L	L	L	L
Initial Inherent Risk – Purchases	E-181	M		M	M	H
Initial Inherent Risk – Cash Payments		M		M	L	M
Initial Inherent Risk – Accounts Payable		L	M	L	L	H
Planned Control Risk – Purchases	E-182					
Planned Control Risk – Cash Payments						
Planned Control Risk – Accounts Payable						
Planned Detection Risk – Purchases	E-183					
Planned Detection Risk – Cash Payments						
Planned Detection Risk – Accounts Payable						

Planned Inherent Risk should be assessed as:
  High (H) unless the combination of inherent risk factors present justify a lower assessment.
  Moderate (M) if the combination of inherent risk factors present justify this assessment.
  Low (L) if the combination of inherent risk factors present justify this assessment.
Factors justifying a lower inherent risk assessment are:
  High management integrity, Low motivation to materially misstate for external parties, Repeat engagement, No material prior year misstatements, No related party transactions, Routine transactions, Limited judgement required to correctly record transactions, Low susceptibility to defalcation, Stable business environment.

Planned Control Risk should be assessed as:
  Low (L) if control activity(ies) reduces the likelihood of a material misstatement to a negligible level and persuasive tests of controls are planned.
  Moderate (M) if control activity(ies) reduces the likelihood of a material misstatement to a negligible level and moderately persuasive tests of controls are planned or control activity(ies) reduces the likelihood of a material misstatement to a moderate level and persuasive tests of controls are planned.
  High (H) if control activity(ies) does not reduce the likelihood of a material misstatement to a reasonable level or no tests of controls are planned.

Planned Detection Risk should be assessed as:
  Low (L) if persuasive substantive tests are planned.
  Moderate (M) if moderately persuasive substantive tests are planned.
  High (H) if minimal substantive tests are planned.

Note: * completeness for cash payments, ** existence for cash payments

The Winery at Chateau Americana	Reference: _E-181_
Expenditure Cycle - Comments Planned Inherent	Prepared by: _JG_
Risk Assessment	Date: _11/13/XX_
For the Year Ended December 31, 20XX	Reviewed by: _____

Comments:

The inherent risk assessment for the existence, valuation, and presentation and disclosure assertions for purchases is set at a moderate level even though no misstatements were identified in prior year audit schedules because of the high volume and variable nature of purchased items and this is a first time engagement.

The inherent risk assessment for the completeness assertion for purchases is set at a high level even though no misstatements were identified in prior year audit schedules because of the external incentives for management to understate this account and this is a first time engagement.

The inherent risk assessment for the existence, valuation, and completeness assertion for cash payments is set at a moderate level even though no misstatements were identified in prior year audit schedules because of the high volume of transactions and this is a first time engagement.

The inherent risk assessment for the presentation and disclosure for cash payments is set at a low level as no misstatements were identified in prior year audit schedules and the recording of cash payments is routine and straight forward.

The inherent risk assessment for the existence, valuation, and presentation and disclosure for accounts payable is set at a low level as no misstatements were identified in prior year audit schedules and the recording of accounts payable transactions is routine and straight forward.

The inherent risk assessment for the rights and obligations for accounts payable is set at a moderate level even though no misstatements were identified in prior year audit schedules because of the motivation for employees to purchase items for their own personal use and this is a first time engagement.

The inherent risk assessment for the completeness for accounts payable is set at a high level even though not misstatements were identified in prior year audit schedules due to the external incentive for management to understate this account and this is a first time engagement.

The Winery at Chateau Americana
Expenditure Cycle - Comments Planned Control
    Risk Assessment
For the Year Ended December 31, 20XX

Reference: *E-182*
Prepared by: _____
Date: _____
Reviewed by: _____

Comments:

The Winery at Chateau Americana
Expenditure Cycle - Comments Planned Detection
    Risk Assessment
For the Year Ended December 31, 20XX

Reference: _E-183_
Prepared by: _____
Date: _____
Reviewed by: _____

Comments:

PERFORMANCE OF AUDIT TESTS FOR THE REVENUE CYCLE (SALES AND CASH COLLECTIONS): The Winery At Chateau Americana

LEARNING OBJECTIVES

After completing and discussing this case, you should be able to:

- Recognize common documents and records used with sales and cash collections
- Recognize common control activities used to process sales and cash collection transactions
- Link client control activities, tests of controls, and substantive tests to management assertions for sales, cash collections, and accounts receivable
- Link client control activities, tests of controls, and substantive tests to risk assessments for sales, cash collections, and accounts receivable
- Perform tests of controls and substantive tests for revenue cycle accounts
- Evaluate the results of tests of controls and substantive tests related to revenue cycle accounts using a non-statistical approach

INTRODUCTION

Chateau Americana (CA) produces and sells premium wines targeted to upscale wine drinkers with retail prices ranging from $10 to $35 per bottle of wine. This year CA sold approximately 385,000 cases of wines. The direct sale and distribution of wine to end consumers is generally not permitted by state regulations. Therefore, CA relies on a network of distributors to sell its wines to consumers. CA currently has agreements with distributors to sell its wines in over 20 state jurisdictions. Most agreements are with small to midsize distributors with a few agreements with large distributors. At the moment, CA does not have any sales agreements with large supermarket chains. No distributor accounts for more than five percent of CA's total sales. Last year, CA had net sales of approximately $22 million.

BACKGROUND INFORMATION ABOUT THE AUDIT

CA has the following general ledger accounts related to sales and cash collection activities

- Sales
- Sales Discounts
- Sales Returns and Allowances
- Bad Debt Expense
- Accounts Receivable
- Allowance for Bad Debts

Julia Granger, audit staff, reviewed CA's policies and procedures related to sales and cash collection activities and prepared the enclosed flowcharts (referenced in the top right hand corner as *R-110, R-111, R-112,*and *R-113*) and planned control risk matrix (audit schedule *R-180*). As a result of this process, Julia developed the enclosed audit program (audit schedules *R-101, R-102, R-103, R-104*). The audit program was approved by Mikel Frucella, audit manager, and Claire Helton, audit partner. The two staff auditors assigned to this engagement are Julia Granger and you. Together, you and Julia are responsible for performing the tests of transactions and test of balances outlined in the revenue cycle audit program (audit schedules *R-101, R-102, R-103,* and *R-104*).

Julia Grainger has already selected the audit samples for the tests of transactions and tests of balances and completed audit procedures 2 through 13 and 15 through 17. Her work is documented on various audit schedules provided in this case.

REQUIREMENTS

You have been assigned responsibility for completing audit steps 1a-b, 14a-b, and 18 listed on audit program *R-101, R-103,* and *R-104.* You will want to review the flowcharts on audit schedules *R-110, R-111, R-112,* and *R-113* to become familiar with the accounting documents and records used with sales and cash collections. Assume you have tested 25 of the 30 sample items selected for audit steps 1a-b. Also assume you have tested 15 of the 20 sample items selected for audit steps 14a-b. No deviations or misstatements were observed for these sample items. The accounting documents and records related to the remaining five sample items for audit steps 1a-c and 14a-b are provided behind the audit schedules. The audit firm has a policy of using the same audit sample for planned tests of controls and substantive tests of transactions (dual-purpose tests) whenever possible to maximize audit efficiency. Thus, the results of the test-of-controls aspect of audit steps 1a-c should be documented on audit schedule *R-410*, whereas the substantive test aspect should be documented on audit schedule *R-440*. The results of the test of balances should be documented on audit schedule *R-520*. Adjusting entries should be proposed on schedule *R-210* for any observed misstatements. You should assume that there was no systematic pattern or intent to commit a fraud based on a review and discussion with client personnel concerning observed deviations and misstatements. Finally, you may want to review the audit schedules already completed by Julia Grainger to have an idea of how each audit step is to be documented.

The Winery at Chateau Americana
Revenue Cycle Audit Program

For the Year Ended December 31, 20XX

Reference: *R-101*
Prepared by: *JG*
Date: *2/18/XY*
Reviewed by: _____

Audit Procedures	Initial	Date	A/S Ref.
1. Select a sample of 30 transactions recorded in the sales register throughout the year and perform the following:	JG	2/16/XY	R-310
a. Examine purchase orders, shipping documents, and sales invoices for authenticity and reasonableness.		✓	R-410 R-440
b. Determine if the sales register amounts were correct based on the sales invoice and shipping document.		✓	R-410 R-440
c. Determine if the sales amounts were posted to the correct customer's accounts receivable master file.	JG	2/17/XY	R-410 R-440
2. Reconcile sales recorded in the sales register to sales and accounts receivable recorded in the general ledger for the month of November.	JG	2/17/XY	R-420
3. Scan the monthly sales registers for large, unusual, or related party transactions and perform follow-up procedures for each one identified.	JG	2/17/XY	R-430
4. Select a sample of 30 shipping documents issued throughout the year and perform the following:	JG	2/16/XY	R-311
a. Obtain the related sales invoice and customer purchase order and determine if shipping document was properly accounted for in the sales register.	JG	2/17/XY	R-411 R-440
5. Inquire and observe the office receptionist open mail in the presence of one other CA employee.	JG	2/18/XY	R-400
6. Inquire and observe the office receptionist prepare a cash summary in the presence of one other CA employee.	JG	2/18/XY	R-400

page . 9S

The Winery at Chateau Americana
Revenue Cycle Audit Program

For the Year Ended December 31, 20XX

Reference: _R-102_
Prepared by: _JG_
Date: _2/19/XY_
Reviewed by: _____

Audit Procedures	Initial	Date	A/S Ref.
7. Select a sample of 30 transactions recorded in the cash receipts journal throughout the year and perform the following:	JG	2/16/XY	R-312
a. Examine validated bank deposit slip and cash receipt summary for authenticity and reasonableness.	JG	2/18/XY	R-412 R-441
b. Determine if the cash receipts journal amounts were correct based on the validated deposit slip and cash receipt summary.	JG	2/18/XY	R-412 R-441
c. Determine if the cash collection amounts were posted to the correct customer's accounts receivable master file.	JG	2/18/XY	R-412 R-441
8. Reconcile cash receipts recorded in the cash receipts journal to cash and accounts receivable recorded in the general ledger for the month of March.	JG	2/18/XY	R-421
9. Scan the monthly cash receipts journal for large, unusual, or related party transactions and perform follow-up procedures for each one identified.	JG	2/18/XY	R-431
10. Select a sample of 30 cash summaries prepared throughout the year and perform the following:	JG	2/16/XY	R-313
a. Obtain the related validated deposit slip and determine if cash collection was properly accounted for in the cash receipts journal.	JG	2/19/XY	R-413 R-441
11. Scan the general journal for the write-off of specific customer accounts and examine credit memo and other supporting documents for customer write-offs greater than $1,000.	JG	2/19/XY	R-432
12. Obtain a lead schedule for revenue cycle accounts and perform the following:	JG	2/16/XY	R-200
a. Agree the prior year balances to prior year audit schedules.	JG	2/16/XY	R-200
b. Agree current year balances to the general ledger.	JG	2/16/XY	R-200

The Winery at Chateau Americana
Revenue Cycle Audit Program

Reference: _R-103_
Prepared by: _JG_
Date: _2/20/XY_
Reviewed by: _____

For the Year Ended December 31, 20XX

Audit Procedures	Initial	Date	A/S Ref.
13. Obtain an aged trial balance printout of year-end customer accounts receivable balances and perform the following:	JG	1/02/XY	N/A
a. Foot the year-end aged trial balance and agree amount to the general ledger and lead schedule.	JG	2/16/XY	R-200
b. Scan the year-end aged trial balance for unusual, related party or credit balances and perform follow-up procedures for each one identified.	JG	2/19/XY	R-511
c. Test the aging of the aged accounts receivable trial balance by examining supporting sales documents for five customers.	JG	2/20/XY	R-500
d. Inquire of the office manager concerning large old outstanding receivable balances.	JG	2/20/XY	R-501
e. Obtain the last 5 bill of ladings issued before year-end and determine if they were properly included in the year-end customer ledgers and aged trial balance printout.	JG	2/20/XY	R-502
f. Obtain the first 5 bill of ladings issued after year-end and determine if they were properly excluded from the year-end customer ledgers and aged trial balance printout.	JG	2/20/XY	R-502
14. Select a sample of the 20 largest customer balances from the aged trial balance and perform the following:	JG	1/02/XY	R-314
a. Confirm the balances directly with the customers using positive confirmations.		✓	R-520
b. Examine documentation supporting subsequent cash collections for positive confirmations not returned.		N/A	R-520
15. Perform the following analytical procedures:			
a. Compare accounts receivable turnover to prior year results.	JG	2/20/XY	R-510
b. Compare the percent aging of accounts receivable to prior year results.	JG	2/20/XY	R-510
b. Compare the allowance for bad debts as a percent of accounts receivable to prior year results.	JG	2/20/XY	R-510

The Winery at Chateau Americana
Revenue Cycle Audit Program

For the Year Ended December 31, 20XX

Reference:	R-104
Prepared by:	JG
Date:	3/05/XY
Reviewed by:	

Audit Procedures	Initial	Date	A/S Ref.
16. Review board of directors' meeting minutes for indication of the factoring or pledging of accounts receivable.	JG	3/05/XY	R-503
17. Inquire of management concerning the:			
a) Factoring or pledging of receivables.	JG	3/05/XY	R-503
b) Existence of related party and/or noncurrent receivables.	JG	3/05/XY	R-503
18. Conclude as to the fair presentation of revenue cycle accounts in all material respects.			R-200

The Winery at Chateau Americana
Revenue Cycle - Sales Flowchart

For the Year Ended December 31, 20XX

Reference:	*R-110*
Prepared by:	*JG*
Date:	*11/14/XX*
Reviewed by:	

Sales Department

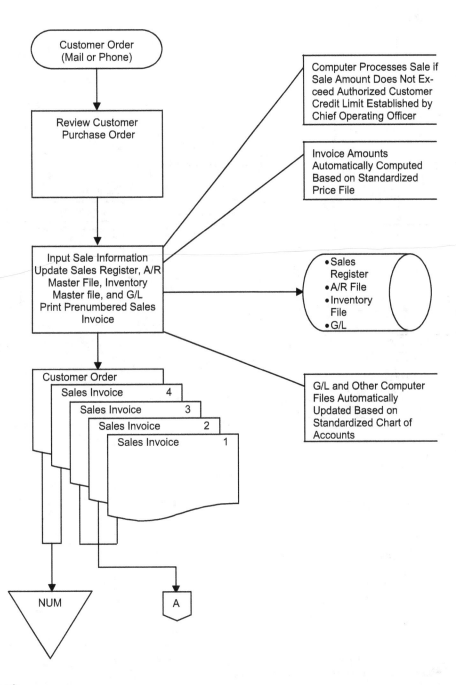

Legend:
NUM - filed numerically by Sales Invoice number
A - off-page connector

The Winery at Chateau Americana
Revenue Cycle - Sales Flowchart

For the Year Ended December 31, 20XX

Reference:	*R-111*
Prepared by:	*JG*
Date:	*11/14/XX*
Reviewed by:	

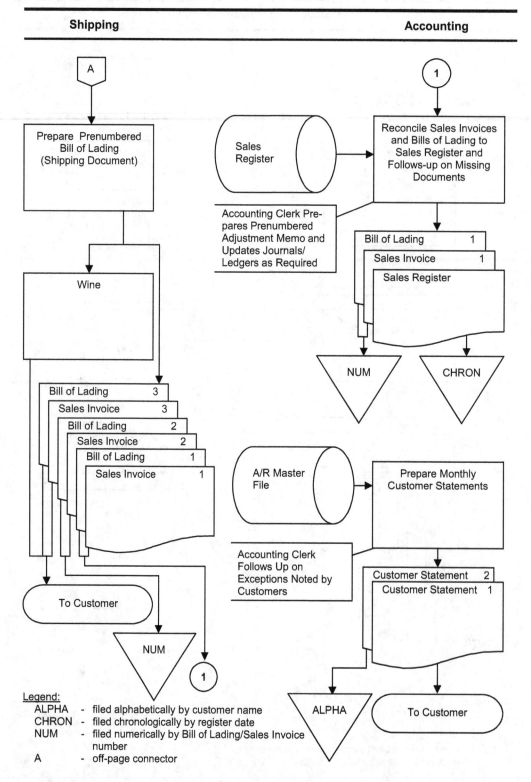

Shipping

Accounting

Prepare Prenumbered Bill of Lading (Shipping Document)

Sales Register

Reconcile Sales Invoices and Bills of Lading to Sales Register and Follows-up on Missing Documents

Accounting Clerk Prepares Prenumbered Adjustment Memo and Updates Journals/Ledgers as Required

Wine

Bill of Lading 1
Sales Invoice 1
Sales Register

NUM   CHRON

Bill of Lading 3
Sales Invoice 3
Bill of Lading 2
Sales Invoice 2
Bill of Lading 1
Sales Invoice 1

A/R Master File

Prepare Monthly Customer Statements

Accounting Clerk Follows Up on Exceptions Noted by Customers

Customer Statement 2
Customer Statement 1

To Customer

NUM

1

ALPHA   To Customer

Legend:
ALPHA - filed alphabetically by customer name
CHRON - filed chronologically by register date
NUM - filed numerically by Bill of Lading/Sales Invoice number
A - off-page connector

The Winery at Chateau Americana
Revenue Cycle - Cash Receipts Flowchart

For the Year Ended December 31, 20XX

Reference: *R-112*
Prepared by: *JG*
Date: *11/14/XX*
Reviewed by:

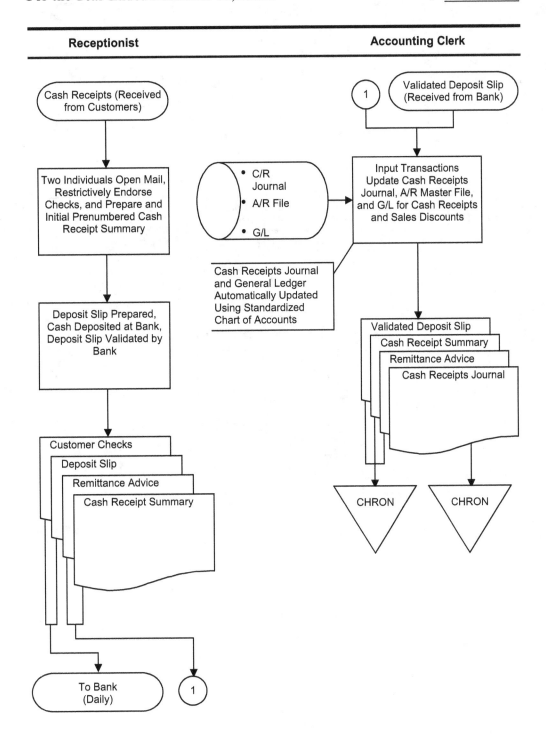

Legend:
CHRON - filed chronologically by summary/journal date.

Ingraham / Jenkins

The Winery at Chateau Americana
Revenue Cycle - Cash Receipts Flowchart

For the Year Ended December 31, 20XX

Reference: _R-113_
Prepared by: _JG_
Date: _11/14/XX_
Reviewed by: _____

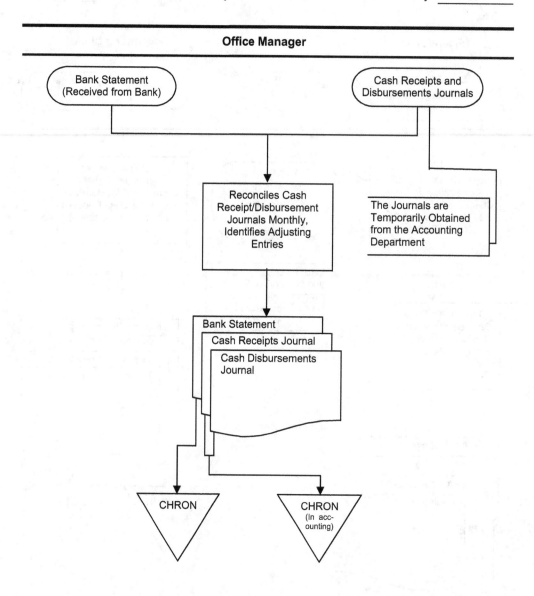

The Winery at Chateau Americana
Revenue Cycle – Planned Audit Risk Matrix

Year Ended December 31, 20XX

Reference:	_R-180_
Prepared by:	_JG_
Date:	_11/14/XX_
Reviewed by:	

	Reference	Existence*	Rights /Obligations	Valuation	Presentation/Disclosure	Completeness**
Tolerable Misstatement: _$40,000, G6_						
Acceptable Audit Risk	G5	L	L	L	L	L
Initial Inherent Risk – Sales		M		M	L	H
Initial Inherent Risk – Cash Collections		H		H	L	H
Initial Inherent Risk – Accounts Receivables		M	L	M	L	L
Planned Control Risk – Sales		M		M	H	M
Planned Control Risk – Cash Collections		M		M	H	M
Planned Detection Risk – Sales		M		M	M	M
Planned Detection Risk – Cash Collections		M		M	M	M
Planned Detection Risk – Accounts Receivable		M	M	M	M	M

Planned Inherent Risk should be assessed as:
  High (H) unless the combination of inherent risk factors present justify a lower assessment.
  Medium (M) if the combination of inherent risk factors present justify this assessment.
  Low (L) if the combination of inherent risk factors present justify this assessment.
Factors justifying a lower inherent risk assessment are:
  High management integrity, Low motivation to materially misstate for external parties,
  Repeat engagement, No material prior year misstatements, No related party transactions,
  Routine transactions, Limited judgement required to correctly record transactions, Low
  susceptibility to defalcation, Stable business environment.

Planned Control Risk should be assessed as:
  Low (L) if control activity(ies) reduces the likelihood of a material misstatement to a
    negligible level and persuasive tests of controls are planned.
  Medium (M) if control activity(ies) reduces the likelihood of a material misstatement to a
    negligible level and moderately persuasive tests of controls are planned or control
    activity(ies) reduces the likelihood of a material misstatement to a moderate level and
    persuasive tests of controls are planned.
  High (H) if control activity(ies) does not reduce the likelihood of a material misstatement to
    a reasonable level or no tests of controls are planned.

Planned Detection Risk should be assessed as:
  Low (L) if persuasive substantive tests are planned.
  Medium (M) if moderately persuasive substantive tests are planned.
  High (H) if minimal substantive tests are planned.

Note: * completeness for cash collections, ** existence for cash collections

Ingraham / Jenkins

The Winery at Chateau Americana
Revenue Cycle - Lead Schedule

For the Year Ended December 31, 20XX

Account	Audited Balance 12/31/XW	Unaudited Balance 12/31/XX	Adjustments Debit	Adjustments Credit	Adjusted Balance 12/31/XX
Accounts Receivable	$ 4,913,697 ✓	$ 5,347,094 f, GL	420	13,400 5800	10,948 = 104,375
Allowance for Bad Debts	$97,460 ✓	$106,375 GL	—	—	
Net Sales	$ 20,189,194 ✓	$ 21,945,422 GL	5800 5460	420	21,939,942
Bad Debt Expense	$9,957 ✓	$10,974 GL	13,400		24,482

5,328,146

Conclusion:

The results of audit tests show that AR,
Allowance for BD, Net Sales, & BD Expense
are fairly stated in all material respects.

Tickmark Legend
✓ - Agreed to prior year audit schedules without exception (audit step 12a).
GL - Agreed to 12/31/20XX general ledger without exception (audit step 12b).
f - Agreed to the footed balance of the 12/31/20XX accounts receivable customer
     ledgers and 12/31/20XX aged accounts receivable trial balance without
     exception (audit step 13a).

The Winery at Chateau Americana
Revenue Cycle - Proposed Adjusting Entry Schedule

For the Year Ended December 31, 20XX

Reference: _R-210_
Prepared by: _JG_
Date: _2/20/XY_
Reviewed by: _____

Account	Debit	Credit
dr. Bad debt expense	$13,488	
cr. Accounts receivable		$13,488
Explanation: *To eliminate the uncollectible receivable balance of $13,488 from accounts receivable while still maintaining an allowance for bad debts balance of 2% of A/R (see R-501).*		
Accounts receivable	420	
Sales revenue		420
Explanation: To correct understated revenue.		
Sales Revenue	5890	
A/R		5890
Explanation: To correct overstated revenue & reflect the wine returned.		
Explanation:		

The Winery at Chateau Americana
Tests of Transactions Sample Plan –
Revenue Cycle Sales Transactions
For the Year Ended December 31, 20XX

Reference:	*R-310*
Prepared by:	*JG*
Date:	*2/16/XY*
Reviewed by:	

Sampling Frame	Beg. Doc. # or Page #	End. Doc. # or Page #	Sample Size
Lines recorded in the sales register during the year	*Page 1 (Line 1)*	*Page 166 (Line 1,992)*	*30*

Sample Selection Method:

The sample was selected by using the "=randbetween(1,1992)" Microsoft Excel spreadsheet function. Line numbers drawn twice were discarded and a new line number was selected using the Excel "randbetween" function.

Sample: *Line number starting with line 1 on page 1 to line 1,992 on page 166*

Sample Item	Sample Ref.	Sample Item	Sample Ref.	Sample Item	Sample Ref.	Sample Item	Sample Ref.
1	*4*	*16*	*904*				
2	*43*	*17*	*908*				
3	*111*	*18*	*945*				
4	*148*	*19*	*960*				
5	*154*	*20*	*1077*				
6	*276*	*21*	*1241*				
7	*311*	*22*	*1284*				
8	*348*	*23*	*1381*				
9	*435*	*24*	*1561*				
10	*444*	*25*	*1633*				
11	*459*	*26*	*1756*				
12	*560*	*27*	*1757*				
13	*657*	*28*	*1821*				
14	*716*	*29*	*1906*				
15	*767*	*30*	*1985*				

The Winery at Chateau Americana
Tests of Transactions Sample Plan -
Revenue Cycle Sales Transactions
For the Year Ended December 31, 20XX

Reference: *R-311*
Prepared by: *JG*
Date: *2/16/XY*
Reviewed by: _____

Sampling Frame	Beg. Doc. # or Page #	End. Doc. # or Page #	Sample Size
Bill of ladings (shipping documents) issued during the year	*134617*	*136608*	*30*

Sample selection method:

The sample items were selected by using the "=randbetween (134617,136608)" Microsoft Excel spreadsheet function. Bill of ladings drawn twice were discarded and a new random number was selected using the Excel "randbetween" function.

Sample: *Bill of Lading Number*

Sample Item	Sample Ref.	Sample Item	Sample Ref.	Sample Item	Sample Ref.	Sample Item	Sample Ref.
1	134628	16	135449				
2	134657	17	135467				
3	134687	18	135675				
4	134711	19	135785				
5	134776	20	135980				
6	134846	21	136245				
7	134942	22	136260				
8	134949	23	136266				
9	134950	24	136356				
10	135111	25	136378				
11	135114	26	136421				
12	135251	27	136425				
13	135329	28	136528				
14	135358	29	136637				
15	135382	30	136728				

The Winery at Chateau Americana
Tests of Transactions Sample Plan -
   Revenue Cycle Cash Receipts
For the Year Ended December 31, 20XX

Reference: *R-312*
Prepared by: *JG*
Date: *2/16/XY*
Reviewed by: _____

Sampling Frame	Beg. Doc. # or Page #	End. Doc. # or Page #	Sample Size
Lines recorded in the cash receipt journal during the year	*Page 1 (Line 1)*	*Page 178 (Line 2,133)*	*30*

Sample Selection Method:

The sample was selected by using the "=randbetween(1,2133)" Microsoft Excel spreadsheet function. Line numbers drawn twice were discarded and a new line number was selected using the Excel "randbetween" function.

Sample: *Line number starting with line 1 on page 1 to line 2,133 on page 178*

Sample Item	Sample Ref.	Sample Item	Sample Ref.	Sample Item	Sample Ref.	Sample Item	Sample Ref.
1	*69*	*16*	*1152*				
2	*86*	*17*	*1157*				
3	*98*	*18*	*1226*				
4	*364*	*19*	*1351*				
5	*387*	*20*	*1387*				
6	*526*	*21*	*1424*				
7	*563*	*22*	*1435*				
8	*622*	*23*	*1458*				
9	*827*	*24*	*1466*				
10	*831*	*25*	*1545*				
11	*859*	*26*	*1679*				
12	*900*	*27*	*1755*				
13	*985*	*28*	*1758*				
14	*1000*	*29*	*1920*				
15	*1048*	*30*	*2091*				

The Winery at Chateau Americana
Nonstatistical Tests of Transactions Sample Plan -
Revenue Cycle Cash Receipt Transactions
For the Year Ended December 31, 20XX

Reference: _R-313_
Prepared by: _JG_
Date: _2/16/XY_
Reviewed by: _____

Sampling Frame	Beg. Doc. # or Page #	End. Doc. # or Page #	Sample Size
Cash receipt summaries prepared during the year	_5468_	_5719_	_30_

Sample selection method:

The sample items were selected by using the "=randbetween(5468,6179)" Microsoft Excel spreadsheet function. Cash summary sheets drawn twice were discarded and a new random number was selected using the Excel "randbetween" function.

Sample: _Cash Receipt Summary Sheet Number_

Sample Item	Sample Ref.	Sample Item	Sample Ref.	Sample Item	Sample Ref.	Sample Item	Sample Ref.
_1_	_5473_	_16_	_5593_				
_2_	_5483_	_17_	_5616_				
_3_	_5484_	_18_	_5618_				
_4_	_5487_	_19_	_5619_				
_5_	_5494_	_20_	_5624_				
_6_	_5515_	_21_	_5646_				
_7_	_5519_	_22_	_5653_				
_8_	_5520_	_23_	_5663_				
_9_	_5525_	_24_	_5666_				
_10_	_5534_	_25_	_5671_				
_11_	_5535_	_26_	_5675_				
_12_	_5538_	_27_	_5692_				
_13_	_5552_	_28_	_5695_				
_14_	_5558_	_29_	_5712_				
_15_	_5569_	_30_	_5714_				

The Winery at Chateau Americana
Nonstatistical Tests of Transactions Sample Plan -
Revenue Cycle Sales Transactions
For the Year Ended December 31, 20XX

Reference:	R-314
Prepared by:	JG
Date:	1/02/XY
Reviewed by:	

Sampling Frame	Beg. Doc. # or Page #	End. Doc. # or Page #	Sample Size
Lines recorded on the aged accounts receivable trial balance	*Page 1 (Line 1)*	*Page 2 (Line 81)*	*20*

Sample Selection Method:

The sample was selected by taking the 20 customers with the largest outstanding balances at year-end.

Sample: Customer *line number starting with line 1 on page 1 to line 81 on page 2*

Sample Item	Sample Ref.	Sample Item	Sample Ref.	Sample Item	Sample Ref.	Sample Item	Sample Ref.	Sample Item	Sample Ref.
1	*0501*	*16*	*3502*						
2	*0502*	*17*	*3801*						
3	*0504*	*18*	*3803*						
4	*0701*	*19*	*4301*						
5	*0901*	*20*	*4601*						
6	*0902*								
7	*1001*								
8	*1301*								
9	*2001*								
10	*2101*								
11	*2201*								
12	*3001*								
13	*3201*								
14	*3302*								
15	*3501*								

The Winery at Chateau Americana
Tests of Transactions -
    Revenue Cycle Cash Receipt Transactions
For the Year Ended December 31, 20XX

Reference:	*R-400*
Prepared by:	*JG*
Date:	*2/18/XY*
Reviewed by:	

Procedure:
Observations and inquires were made of the office receptionist regarding the handling of cash receipt mail and preparation of cash summary sheets. Consistent with established company policy, cash receipt envelopes are always opened by the office receptionist in the presence of one other company employee and the cash receipt is immediately recorded on a cash summary sheet.
Exceptions/Misstatements Identified:
No exceptions or misstatements were noted as a result of performing audit
procedures 5 and 6.
Follow-up procedures performed:
No follow-up procedures are necessary.

Ingraham / Jenkins

The Winery at Chateau Americana
Nonstatistical Tests of Controls Evaluation –
Revenue Cycle Sales Transactions
For the Year Ended December 31, 20XX

Sampling Frame: *Lines recorded in the sales register during the year*

Attribute	RCL	Sample Size	SDR	TDR	ASR
Purchase order, shipping document, and sales invoice look authentic and reasonable.	M	30	0%	5%	5%
Sales register amount is correct based on sales invoice and shipping document.	M	30	3.3%	5%	1.7%
Sales invoice is posted to correct customer's accounts receivable master file.	M	30	0%	5%	5%

Conclusion: There was only one deviation. Everything here is good b/c our tolerable rate is 5% & the sampling deviation rate is below that amount.

Legend:
ASR - Allowance for Sampling Risk (TDR-SDR)
RCL - Risk of Assessing Control Risk Too Low (L – Low or M – Moderate)
SDR - Sample Deviation Rate
TDR - Tolerable Deviation Rate

The Winery at Chateau Americana
Nonstatistical Tests of Controls Evaluation -
Revenue Cycle Sales Transactions
For the Year Ended December 31, 20XX

Reference: *R-411*
Prepared by: *JG*
Date: *2/17/XY*
Reviewed by: _____

Sampling Frame: *Bill of ladings (shipping documents) issued during the year*					
Attribute	**RCL**	**Sample Size**	**SDR**	**TDR**	**ASR**
Bill of lading is properly accounted for in sales register.	*M*	*30*	*0%*	*5%*	*5%*

Conclusion:

The results of audit procedure 4a support a reduced control risk assessment for the completeness and valuation of sales as no deviations from company policy were noted. Therefore, no changes to the planned audit program are required.

Legend:
ASR - Allowance for Sampling Risk (TDR-SDR)
RCL - Risk of Assessing Control Risk Too Low (L – Low or M – Moderate)
SDR - Sample Deviation Rate
TDR - Tolerable Deviation Rate

The Winery at Chateau Americana
Nonstatistical Tests of Controls Evaluation -
   Revenue Cycle Cash Receipts
For the Year Ended December 31, 20XX

Reference:	*R-412*
Prepared by:	*JG*
Date:	*2/18/XY*
Reviewed by:	

Sampling Frame: *Lines recorded in the cash receipt journal during the year*

Attribute	RCL	Sample Size	SDR	TDR	ASR
Validated bank deposit slip and cash summary sheet look authentic and reasonable.	*M*	*30*	*0%*	*5%*	*5%*
Cash receipt journal amount is correct based on deposit slip and cash summary sheet.	*M*	*30*	*0%*	*5%*	*5%*
Cash collection amount is posted to correct customers accounts receivable master file.	*M*	*30*	*0%*	*5%*	*5%*

Conclusion:

The results of audit procedures 7a, b, and c support a reduced control risk assessment for the existence and valuation of cash receipts as no deviations from company policy were noted. Therefore, no changes to the planned audit program are required.

Legend:
ASR - Allowance for Sampling Risk (TDR-SDR)
RCL - Risk of Assessing Control Risk Too Low (L – Low or M – Moderate)
SDR - Sample Deviation Rate
TDR - Tolerable Deviation Rate

The Winery at Chateau Americana
Nonstatistical Tests of Controls Evaluation -
  Revenue Cycle Cash Receipts
For the Year Ended December 31, 20XX

Reference: _R-413_
Prepared by: _JG_
Date: _2/19/XY_
Reviewed by: _____

Sampling Frame: Cash summary sheets prepared *during the year*

Attribute	RCL	Sample Size	SDR	TDR	ASR
Cash summary sheet is properly accounted for in cash receipt journal.	*M*	*30*	*0%*	*5%*	*5%*

Follow-up procedures performed:

The results of audit procedure 10a support a reduced control risk assessment for the completeness and valuation of cash receipts as no deviations from company policy were noted. Therefore, no changes to the planned audit program are required.

Legend:
ASR - Allowance for Sampling Risk (TDR-SDR)
RCL - Risk of Assessing Control Risk Too Low (L – Low or M – Moderate)
SDR - Sample Deviation Rate
TDR - Tolerable Deviation Rate

The Winery at Chateau Americana
Tests of Transactions -
  Revenue Cycle Sales Transactions
For the Year Ended December 31, 20XX

Reference:	*R-420*
Prepared by:	*JG*
Date:	*2/17/XY*
Reviewed by:	

Procedure:

Sales recorded in the sales register were reconciled to sales and accounts receivable recorded in the general ledger for the month of November.

Exceptions/Misstatements Identified:

No exceptions or misstatements were noted as a result of performing audit

procedure 2.

Follow-up procedures performed:

No follow-up procedures are necessary.

The Winery at Chateau Americana
Tests of Transactions -
Revenue Cycle Cash Receipt Transactions
For the Year Ended December 31, 20XX

Reference: *R-421*
Prepared by: *JG*
Date: *2/18/XY*
Reviewed by: _____

Procedure:
Cash receipts recorded in the cash receipts journal were reconciled to cash and accounts receivable recorded in the general ledger for the month of March.

Exceptions/Misstatements Identified:
No exceptions or misstatements were noted as a result of performing audit
procedure 8.

Follow-up procedures performed:
No follow-up procedures are necessary.

The Winery at Chateau Americana
Unusual Transactions - Revenue Cycle
   Sales Register
For the Year Ended December 31, 20XX

	Reference:	R-430
	Prepared by:	JG
	Date:	2/17/XY
	Reviewed by:	

Date	Account Description or Customer of Unusual Transactions Identified	Ref.	Account IDs	Amount
	No unusual transactions identified.			

Follow-up procedures performed:

No follow-up procedures are necessary.

The Winery at Chateau Americana
Unusual Transactions - Revenue Cycle
   Cash Receipts Journal
For the Year Ended December 31, 20XX

Reference: _R-431_
Prepared by: _JG_
Date: _2/18/XY_
Reviewed by: _____

Date	Account Description or Payer of Unusual Transactions Identified	Ref.	Account IDs	Amount
	No unusual transactions identified.			

Conclusion/Follow-up procedures performed:

No follow-up procedures are necessary.

The Winery at Chateau Americana
Unusual Transactions - Revenue Cycle
    General Journal - Customer Write-offs
For the Year Ended December 31, 20XX

Reference: _R-432_
Prepared by: _JG_
Date: _2/19/XY_
Reviewed by: _____

Date	Account Description or Customer of Unusual Transactions Identified	Ref.	Account IDs	Amount
	No unusual transactions identified.			

Follow-up procedures performed:

No follow-up procedures are necessary.

The Winery at Chateau Americana
Nonstatistical Substantive Tests Evaluation –
Revenue Cycle Sales Transactions
For the Year Ended December 31, 20XX

Reference:	*R-440*	
Prepared by:		
Date:		
Reviewed by:		

Misstatements:	Recorded Amount	Audited Amount	Misstatement Amount
Sales journal reports 420 less than the invoice amount for Market Wine	11,566.90	11,986.80	420
Total sample misstatement			420

Projected misstatement:

Total sample misstatement			420
Dollar value of sample		+	$727,107
Percentage sample dollar misstatement		=	0.00058
Dollar value of population per register		×	$21,945,490
Projected population dollar misstatement		=	12,676.41

Allowance for sampling risk

Tolerable misstatement			$40,000
Projected population dollar misstatement		−	12,676
Recorded adjustments		+	420
Allowance for sampling risk		=	27,744

Conclusions:

One misstatement was found. The value of the misstatement is small when compared to total sales + AR. The value of allowance for SR is sufficient to support that sales are is fairly stated in all material respects

The Winery at Chateau Americana	Reference:	R-441
Nonstatistical Substantive Tests Evaluation –	Prepared by:	JG
Revenue Cycle Cash Receipts Transactions	Date:	2/19/XY
For the Year Ended December 31, 20XX	Reviewed by:	

Misstatements:	Recorded Amount	Audited Amount	Misstatement Amount
No missatements were identified as a			
result of performing audit procedures			
7a-c and 10.			
Total sample misstatement			$0

Projected misstatement:		
Total sample misstatement		$0
Dollar value of sample	÷	$ 662,470
Percentage sample dollar misstatement	=	$0
Dollar value of population per journal	×	$25,233,126
Projected population dollar misstatement	=	$0
Allowance for sampling risk		
Tolerable misstatement		$40,000
Projected population dollar misstatement	–	$0
Recorded adjustments	+	$0
Allowance for sampling risk	=	$40,000

Conclusions:

The results of audit procedures 7a-c and 10 support the completeness, existence, valution, and presentation and disclosure of cash receipts in all material respects. Therefore, no changes to the planned audit program are required.

The Winery at Chateau Americana
Tests of Balances – Revenue Cycle
    Accounts Receivable
For the Year Ended December 31, 20XX

Reference:	*R-500*
Prepared by:	*JG*
Date:	*2/20/XY*
Reviewed by:	

Procedure:

The proper aging of the aged accounts receivable trial balance was verified by examining the supporting sales invoices for the following five customers: Blue Ridge Beverage Company, Johnson Brothers Company, Premier Wine and Spirits, Southern Wine and Spirits, Young's Market Company.

Exceptions/Misstatements Identified:

No exceptions or misstatements were noted as a result of performing audit

procedure 13c.

Follow-up procedures performed:

No follow-up procedures are necessary.

The Winery at Chateau Americana
Inquires – Revenue Cycle
    Accounts Receivable
For the Year Ended December 31, 20XX

Reference:	*R-501*
Prepared by:	*JG*
Date:	*2/20/XY*
Reviewed by:	

Inquires of:	*Office Manager*

Question:	Response:
The collectibility of the Fine Wine and Spirits, Inc. receivable balance of $13,488 was discussed with the office manager as it was over a year old.	*Per the office manager, CA has stopped selling to Fine Wine and Spirits because of the lack of payment and has referred the balance to a collection agency. The office manager does not believe the company will collect on this balance.*
The collectibility of the Desert Beverage Company receivable balance of $6,221 was discussed with the office manager as it was almost a year old.	*Per the office manager, CA had negotiated at year-end a payment plan of $1,037 over the next six months starting in January. A review of the January and February 20XY cash receipts reveals that two payments totaling $2,074 were received From Desert Beverage Co. This balance appears collectible.*

Follow-up procedures performed:

No other receivable balances listed on the aged trial balance were identified as unusually large and old. Therefore, no change to the planned audit program is necessary. Based on the discussions with the office manager and analytic procedures performed related to the collection of receivables (see R-510). The following adjusting entry is proposed (see R-210):
    dr. Bad debt expense $13,488
        cr. Accounts receivable $13,488
This entry will eliminate the uncollectible receivable balance of $13,488 from accounts receivable account while still maintaining an allowance for bad debts balance at 2% of accounts receivable.

The Winery at Chateau Americana
Tests of Balances – Revenue Cycle
    Accounts Receivable
For the Year Ended December 31, 20XX

Reference:	*R-502*
Prepared by:	*JG*
Date:	*2/20/XY*
Reviewed by:	

Procedure:

The last bill of lading issued before December 31, 20XX was 136608. The sales invoices and purchase orders supporting the last five bill of ladings issued before year-end and first five bill of ladings issued after year-end were examined and traced to proper inclusion/exclusion in/from the December 31, 20XX accounts receivable customer ledgers.

Exceptions/Misstatements Identified:

No exceptions or misstatements were noted as a result of performing audit

procedures 13e and f.

Follow-up procedures performed:

No follow-up procedures are necessary.

The Winery at Chateau Americana	Reference:	*R-503*
Tests of Balances – Revenue Cycle	Prepared by:	*JG*
Accounts Receivable	Date:	*3/1/XY*
For the Year Ended December 31, 20XX	Reviewed by:	

Procedure:

The board of directors' meeting minutes issued from 1/1/20XX through 3/1/20XY were reviewed for indication of the factoring or pledging of accounts receivable. Additionally, inquiries were made of the chief financial officer concerning the factoring or pledging of receivables and/or the existence of related party/noncurrent receivables.

Exceptions/Misstatements Identified:

No exceptions or misstatements were noted as a result of performing audit

procedures 16, 17a, and 17b.

Follow-up procedures performed:

No follow-up procedures are necessary.

The Winery at Chateau Americana
Ratio Analysis - Revenue Cycle

Reference:	*R-510*	
Prepared by:	*JG*	
Date:	*2/20/XY*	
Reviewed by:		

For the Year Ended December 31, 20XX

Ratio Description	20XX Ratio Amount	20XW Ratio Amount	Conclusion/Follow-up Procedures Performed
Accounts Receivable Turnover	4.36	4.74	Per the office manager the turnover and aging of receivables has worsened slightly as the company started offering more favorable credit terms to select
Percent of Receivables: 0 to 60 days old 61 to 120 days old 121 to 180 days old greater than 181 days old	42.6% 34.9% 15.9% 6.6%	46.8% 34.2% 14.3% 4.7%	customers to encourage higher sales volume. The office manager believes that the allowance for bad debts of $200,000 is sufficient to cover any uncollectible balances.
Allowance for Bad Debts as Percent of Accounts Receivable	2.0%	2.0%	Based on the review of the A/R aged trial balance (see R-501), past history, and current economic conditions the allowance percent of 2% of A/R is reasonable.

The Winery at Chateau Americana
Unusual Transactions - Revenue Cycle Printout of
Aged Accounts Receivable Trial Balance
For the Year Ended December 31, 20XX

Reference: _R-511_
Prepared by: _JG_
Date: _2/19/XY_
Reviewed by: _____

Date	Account Description or Customer of Unusual Transactions Identified	Ref.	Account IDs	Amount
	No unusual transactions identified.			

Follow-up procedures performed:

No follow-up procedures are necessary.

The Winery at Chateau Americana
Nonstatistical Tests of Balance Evaluation –
Revenue Cycle Accounts Receivable
For the Year Ended December 31, 20XX

Reference: _R-520_
Prepared by: _____
Date: _____
Reviewed by: _____

Misstatements:	Recorded Amount	Audited Amount	Misstatement Amount
Shipment of wine returned by vintage wine company is still included in A/R	255,169.80	249,289.80	5880
Total Sample Misstatement			5880

Projected Misstatement:		
Total Sample Misstatement		5880
Dollar Value of Sample	÷	$1,785,704
Percentage Sample Dollar Misstatement	=	.00329
Dollar Value of Population per G/L	×	$5,240,719
Projected Dollar Misstatement for Accounts Receivable	=	17,256.74

Allowance for Sampling Risk		
Tolerable Misstatement		$40,000
Projected Dollar Misstatement for Accounts Receivable	–	17,256.74
Recorded Adjustments	+	5880
Allowance for Sampling Risk	=	28,623.26

Conclusions:

one misstatement was identified. Wine was returned during the period, but not recorded as a return. The amount of the misstatement is small relative to total sales + AR. The allowance for SR is greater than the misstatement. Therefore, it can be concluded that AR is stated fairly in all material respects.

The Winery at Chateau Americana Chart of Accounts			
Account Description	**Account Number**	**Account Description**	**Account Number**
General Checking Account	111000	Sales	410000
Payroll Checking Account	112000	Sales Discounts	420000
Money Market Account	113000	Sales Returns and Allowances	430000
Savings Account	114000	Gains/Loss Marketable Securities	452000
Petty Cash	119000	Dividend Income	491000
Accounts Receivable	121000	Interest Income	492000
Allowance for Bad Debts	129000	Cost of Goods Sold	510000
Inventory- Production	141000	Wages and Salary Expense	601000
Inventory - Finished Goods	145000	Sales Commission Expense	601500
Prepaid Expenses	150000	FICA Tax Expense	602100
Land and Buildings	160000	Medicare Tax Expense	602200
Equipment	170000	FUTA Tax Expense	602300
Accumulated Depreciation	180000	SUTA Tax Expense	602400
Investments	191000	Utilities Expense	611000
Accounts Payable	210000	Irrigation & Waste Disposal	
Federal Income Tax Withheld	222100	Expense	611300
FICA Withheld	222200	Landscaping Expense	612000
Medicare Withheld	222300	Advertising Expense	621000
FICA Payable - Employer	223100	Marketing Expense	623000
Medicare Payable - Employer	223200	Festivals & Competitions Expense	624000
Unemployment Taxes Payable	223300	Telephone Expense	631000
Federal Income Taxes Payable	235000	Internet & Computer Expense	632000
Property Taxes Payable	236000	Postage Expense	633000
Mortgages Payable	240000	Legal & Accounting Fees	641000
Notes Payables	261000	Office Supplies Expense	651000
Common Stock	310000	Data Processing Expense	660000
Paid in Capital Excess Par -		Depreciation Expense	670000
Common	311000	Travel and Entertainment Expense	680000
Dividends - Common	312000	Other Insurance Expense	691000
Retained Earnings	390000	Medical Insurance Expense	692000
		Workmen's Compensation	
		Insurance	693000
		Other Employee Benefit Expense	699000
		Dues and Subscription Expense	700000
		Federal Income Tax Expense	711000
		Property Tax Expense	712000
		Repairs and Maintenance Expense	721000
		Automobile Expense	731000
		Lease Expense	740000
		Bad Dept Expense	791000
		Miscellaneous Expense	792000
		Interest Expense	793000

Note: Pages 95 to 106 contain documentation required to complete two of the open audit procedures shown on the audit program on pages 59 to 62. Document for Audit Procedure 1 is available on pages 95 to 100 and documentation for Audit Procedure 14 is available on pages 101 to 106.

	The Winery at Chateau Americana Sales Register for Audit Procedure 1* For the Period From January 1, 20XX to December 31, 20XX				
Date	G.L. Account ID - Account Description	Customer No.	Invoice No.	Debit Amount	Credit Amount
01/10/XX (43)	121000 - Accounts Receivable 410000 - Sales	0501	13713	16,186.80	16,186.80
03/19/XX (348)	121000 - Accounts Receivable 410000 - Sales	3301	14081	8,373.60	8,373.60
06/12/XX (716)	121000 - Accounts Receivable 410000 - Sales	0901	14386	11,566.80	11,566.80
11/20/XX (1633)	121000 - Accounts Receivable 410000 - Sales	1301	15303	11,444.40	11,444.40
12/11/XX (1821)	121000 - Accounts Receivable 410000 - Sales	3802	15491	10,220.40	10,220.40

(handwritten annotation next to 11,566.80 credit: "< by 420 11,986.80")

*Abstracted from the Sales Register using exact format of the actual Sales Register. Note that the number in parenthesis under the transaction date is not normally included in the Sales Register. This number is provided as it represents the line number of the transaction in the Sales Register.

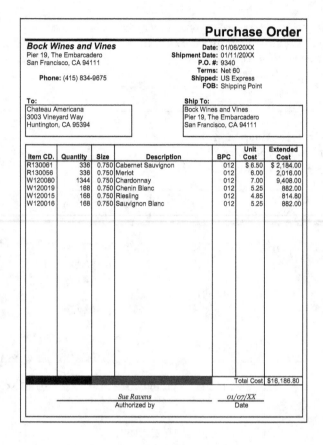

Purchase Order

Bock Wines and Vines
Pier 19, The Embarcadero
San Francisco, CA 94111

Phone: (415) 834-9675

Date: 01/06/20XX
Shipment Date: 01/11/20XX
P.O. #: 9340
Terms: Net 60
Shipped: US Express
FOB: Shipping Point

To:
Chateau Americana
3003 Vineyard Way
Huntington, CA 95394

Ship To:
Bock Wines and Vines
Pier 19, The Embarcadero
San Francisco, CA 94111

Item CD.	Quantity	Size	Description	BPC	Unit Cost	Extended Cost
R130061	336	0.750	Cabernet Sauvignon	012	$ 6.50	$ 2,184.00
R130056	336	0.750	Merlot	012	6.00	2,016.00
W120080	1344	0.750	Chardonnay	012	7.00	9,408.00
W120019	168	0.750	Chenin Blanc	012	5.25	882.00
W120015	168	0.750	Riesling	012	4.85	814.80
W120016	168	0.750	Sauvignon Blanc	012	5.25	882.00

Total Cost $16,186.80

Sue Ravens
Authorized by

_01/07/XX_
Date

CREDIT SALES INVOICE

Invoice Number: 13713

Chateau Americana, Inc.
3003 Vineyard Way
Huntington, CA 95394
(707)368-8485
CA-NC-67

Invoice Date: 01/10/XX

Credit Terms: Net 60

Sold To:
Bock Wines and Vines
Pier 19, The Embarcadero
San Francisco, CA 94111

Ship To:
Bock Wines and Vines
Pier 19, The Embarcadero
San Francisco, CA 94111

Salesperson	Customer P.O. Number	Customer Number	ABC Number
WAB	9340	0501	CA07891

Product	Description	Size	Quantity	Cost	Extended
R130061	Cabernet Sauvignon	0.750	336	$ 6.50	$ 2,184.00
R130056	Merlot	0.750	336	6.00	2,016.00
W120080	Chardonnay	0.750	1344	7.00	9,408.00
W120019	Chenin Blanc	0.750	168	5.25	882.00
W120015	Riesling	0.750	168	4.85	814.80
W120016	Sauvignon Blanc	0.750	168	5.25	882.00

Grand Total Bottles: 2,520
Total Cases: 210
Comments:

Grand Total Cost: $ 16,186.80

Date 01/10/XX
Invoice Number 13713
Customer Number 0501

Distribution: Copy 1 - Accounting; Copy 2 - Shipping; Copy 3 - Customer; Copy 4 - Sales

---

Date 01/10/XX	Uniform Bill of Lading	

Ship From

Name: *Chateau Americana, Inc.*
Address: *3003 Vineyard Way*
City/State/Zip: *Huntington, CA 95394*
SID No.: *122448*

Bill of Lading Number: 134659

Carrier Name: *US Express*

Ship To
Name: *Bock Wines and Vines*
Address: *Pier 19, The Embarcadero*
City/State/Zip: *San Francisco, CA 94111*
CID No.: *244888*

Trailer Number: *KLDF 897*

Serial Number: *000123123*

Special Instructions:

Freight Charge Terms: (Freight charges are prepaid unless marked otherwise)
Prepaid: ☐ Collect: ☒ 3rd Party: ☐
☐ (check box): Master bill of lading with attached underlying bills of lading.

Customer Order Information

Description of Items	Quantity	Weight	Pallet/Slip (circle one)	Additional Shipper Information
Wine	210	7,140	(Y) N	
			Y N	
			Y N	
			Y N	
Grand Total	210	7,140		

Where the rate is dependent on value, shippers are required to state specifically in writing the agreed or declared value of the property as follows: 'The agreed or declared value of the property is specifically stated by the shipper to be not exceeding _____ per _____.

COD Amount: $ _____ N/A
Free Terms:
☐ Collect
☐ Prepaid
☐ Customer check acceptable

Note: Liability limitation for loss or damage in this shipment may be applicable. See 49 USC §14706 (c) (1) (A) & (B)

Received, subject to individually determined rates or contracts that have been agreed upon in writing between the carrier and shipper, if applicable, otherwise to the rates, classifications and rules that have been established by the carrier and are available to the shipper, on request, and to all applicable state and federal regulations.

The carrier shall not make delivery of this shipment without payment of and all other lawful charges.

Shipper Signature _Jerry Richards_

Shipper Signature/Date	Trailer Loaded:	Carrier Signature/Pickup Date

This is to certify that the above named materials are properly classified, packaged, marked and labeled, and are in proper condition for transportation according to the applicable regulations of the DOT.

☐ By shipper
☒ By Driver

Carrier acknowledges receipt of packages and required placards. Carrier certifies emergency response information was made available and/or carrier has the DOT emergency response guidebook or equivalent documentation in the vehicle. Property described above is received in good order, except as noted.

Jerry Richards _01/10/XX_

Frank Loren _01/10/XX_

Distribution: Copy 1 - Accounting; Copy 2 - Shipping; Copy 3- Customer

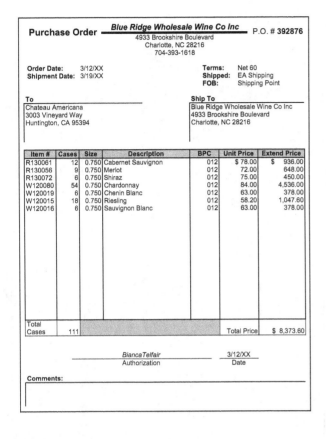

Purchase Order — **Blue Ridge Wholesale Wine Co Inc** P.O. # 392876
4933 Brookshire Boulevard
Charlotte, NC 28216
704-393-1618

Order Date: 3/12/XX
Shipment Date: 3/19/XX

Terms: Net 60
Shipped: EA Shipping
FOB: Shipping Point

To
Chateau Americana
3003 Vineyard Way
Huntington, CA 95394

Ship To
Blue Ridge Wholesale Wine Co Inc
4933 Brookshire Boulevard
Charlotte, NC 28216

Item #	Cases	Size	Description	BPC	Unit Price	Extend Price
R130061	12	0.750	Cabernet Sauvignon	012	$ 78.00	$ 936.00
R130056	9	0.750	Merlot	012	72.00	648.00
R130072	6	0.750	Shiraz	012	75.00	450.00
W120080	54	0.750	Chardonnay	012	84.00	4,536.00
W120019	6	0.750	Chenin Blanc	012	63.00	378.00
W120015	18	0.750	Riesling	012	58.20	1,047.60
W120016	6	0.750	Sauvignon Blanc	012	63.00	378.00

| Total Cases | 111 | | | | Total Price | $ 8,373.60 |

Bianca Telfair   3/12/XX
Authorization   Date

Comments:

CREDIT SALES INVOICE   Invoice Number: **14081**

Chateau Americana, Inc.   Invoice Date: 03/19/XX
3003 Vineyard Way
Huntington, CA 95394   Credit Terms: Net 60
(707)368-8485
CA-NC-67

Sold To:
Blue Ridge Whs Wine Co Inc
4933 Brookshire Boulevard
Charlotte, NC 28216

Ship To:
Blue Ridge Whs Wine Co Inc
4933 Brookshire Boulevard
Charlotte, NC 28216

Salesperson MMM	Customer P.O. Number 392876	Customer Number 3301	ABC Number NC45963

Product	Description	Size	Quantity	Cost	Extended
R130061	Cabernet Sauvignon	0.750	144	$ 6.50	$ 936.00
R130056	Merlot	0.750	108	6.00	648.00
R130072	Shiraz	0.750	72	6.25	450.00
W120080	Chardonnay	0.750	648	7.00	4,536.00
W120019	Chenin Blanc	0.750	72	5.25	378.00
W120015	Riesling	0.750	216	4.85	1,047.60
W120016	Sauvignon Blanc	0.750	72	5.25	378.00

Grand Total Bottles: 1,332   Grand Total Cost: $ 8,373.60

Total Cases: 111
Comments:

Date 03/19/XX
Invoice Number 14081
Customer Number 3301

Distribution: Copy 1 - Accounting; Copy 2 - Shipping; Copy 3 - Customer; Copy 4 - Sales

---

Date 03/19/XX	Uniform Bill of Lading

Ship From

Name: _Chateau Americana, Inc._
Address: 3003 Vineyard Way
City/State/Zip: Huntington, CA 95394
SID No.: 122448

Bill of Lading Number: _____ 134964

Carrier Name: _EA Shipping_

Trailer Number: 7777 SOU

Serial Number: 022323444

Ship To
Name: _Blue Ridge Whs Wine Co Inc_
Address: 4933 Brookshire Boulevard
City/State/Zip: Charlotte, NC 28216
CID No.: 883229

Special Instructions:

Freight Charge Terms: (Freight charges are prepaid unless marked otherwise)
Prepaid: ☐   Collect: ☒   3rd Party: ☐
☐ (check box): Master bill of lading with attached underlying bills of lading.

Customer Order Information

Description of Items	Quantity	Weight	Pallet/Slip (circle one)	Additional Shipper Information
Wine	111	3,774	Ⓨ N	
			Y N	
			Y N	
			Y N	
Grand Total	111	3,774		

COD Amount: $ _____ N/A
Free Terms:
☐ Collect
☐ Prepaid
☐ Customer check acceptable

Where the rate is dependent on value, shippers are required to state specifically in writing the agreed or declared value of the property as follows: "The agreed or declared value of the property is specifically stated by the shipper to be not exceeding _____ per _____."

Note: Liability limitation for loss or damage in this shipment may be applicable. See 49 USC §14706 (c) (1) (A) & (B)

Received, subject to individually determined rates or contracts that have been agreed upon in writing between the carrier and shipper, if applicable, otherwise to the rates, classifications and rules that have been established by the carrier and are available to the shipper, on request, and to all applicable state and federal regulations.

The carrier shall not make delivery of this shipment without payment of and all other lawful charges.

Shipper Signature   _Jerry Richards_

Shipper Signature/Date

This is to certify that the above named materials are properly classified, packaged, marked and labeled, and are in proper condition for transportation according to the applicable regulations of the DOT.

Jerry Richards   03/19/XX

Trailer Loaded:
☐ By shipper
☒ By Driver

Carrier Signature/Pickup Date
Carrier acknowledges receipt of packages and required placards. Carrier certifies emergency response information was made available and/or carrier has the DOT emergency response guidebook or equivalent documentation in the vehicle. Property described above is received in good order, except as noted.

Basi Abbas   03/19/XX

Distribution: Copy 1 - Accounting; Copy 2 - Shipping; Copy 3- Customer

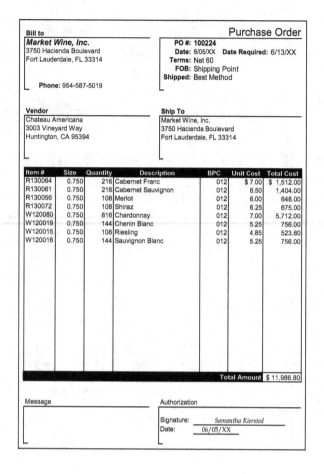

Purchase Order

Bill to
Market Wine, Inc.
3750 Hacienda Boulevard
Fort Lauderdale, FL 33314

Phone: 954-587-5019

PO #: 100224
Date: 6/05/XX Date Required: 6/13/XX
Terms: Net 60
FOB: Shipping Point
Shipped: Best Method

Vendor
Chateau Americana
3003 Vineyard Way
Huntington, CA 95394

Ship To
Market Wine, Inc.
3750 Hacienda Boulevard
Fort Lauderdale, FL 33314

Item #	Size	Quantity	Description	BPC	Unit Cost	Total Cost
R130064	0.750	216	Cabernet Franc	012	$7.00	$ 1,512.00
R130061	0.750	216	Cabernet Sauvignon	012	6.50	1,404.00
R130056	0.750	108	Merlot	012	6.00	648.00
R130072	0.750	108	Shiraz	012	6.25	675.00
W120080	0.750	816	Chardonnay	012	7.00	5,712.00
W120019	0.750	144	Chenin Blanc	012	5.25	756.00
W120015	0.750	108	Riesling	012	4.85	523.80
W120016	0.750	144	Sauvignon Blanc	012	5.25	756.00

Total Amount $ 11,986.80

Message

Authorization

Signature: *Samantha Kiersted*
Date: 06/05/XX

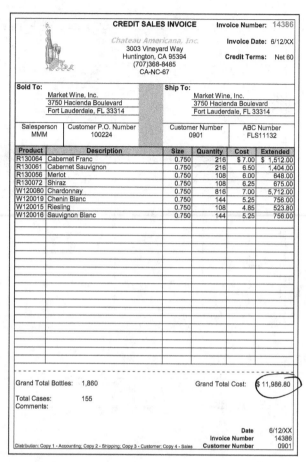

CREDIT SALES INVOICE Invoice Number: 14386

Chateau Americana, Inc.
3003 Vineyard Way
Huntington, CA 95394
(707)368-8485
CA-NC-67

Invoice Date: 6/12/XX
Credit Terms: Net 60

Sold To:
Market Wine, Inc.
3750 Hacienda Boulevard
Fort Lauderdale, FL 33314

Ship To:
Market Wine, Inc.
3750 Hacienda Boulevard
Fort Lauderdale, FL 33314

Salesperson	Customer P.O. Number	Customer Number	ABC Number
MMM	100224	0901	FLS11132

Product	Description	Size	Quantity	Cost	Extended
R130064	Cabernet Franc	0.750	216	$7.00	$ 1,512.00
R130061	Cabernet Sauvignon	0.750	216	6.50	1,404.00
R130056	Merlot	0.750	108	6.00	648.00
R130072	Shiraz	0.750	108	6.25	675.00
W120080	Chardonnay	0.750	816	7.00	5,712.00
W120019	Chenin Blanc	0.750	144	5.25	756.00
W120015	Riesling	0.750	108	4.85	523.80
W120016	Sauvignon Blanc	0.750	144	5.25	756.00

Grand Total Bottles: 1,860

Grand Total Cost: $ 11,986.80

Total Cases: 155
Comments:

Date 6/12/XX
Invoice Number 14386
Customer Number 0901

Distribution: Copy 1 - Accounting; Copy 2 - Shipping; Copy 3 - Customer; Copy 4 - Sales

Date 06/12/XX	Uniform Bill of Lading	

Ship From
Name: Chateau Americana, Inc.
Address: 3003 Vineyard Way
City/State/Zip: Huntington, CA 95394
SID No.: 122448

Bill of Lading Number: 135332

Carrier Name: Crossway Deliveries

Ship To
Name: Market Wine, Inc.
Address: 3750 Hacienda Boulevard
City/State/Zip: Fort Lauderdale, FL 33314
CID No.: 456997

Trailer Number: ABC 3210

Serial Number: 000456789

Special Instructions:

Freight Charge Terms: (Freight charges are prepaid unless marked otherwise)
Prepaid: ☐ Collect: ☑ 3rd Party: ☐
(check box): Master bill of lading with attached underlying bills of lading.

Customer Order Information

Description of Items	Quantity	Weight	Pallet/Slip (circle one)	Additional Shipper Information
Wine	155	5,270	Y N	
			Y N	
			Y N	
			Y N	
Grand Total	155	5,270		

COD Amount: $ _____ N/A
Free Terms:
☐ Collect
☐ Prepaid
☐ Customer check acceptable

Note: Liability limitation for loss or damage in this shipment may be applicable. See 49 USC §14706(1) (A) & (B)

Where the rate is dependent on value, shippers are required to state specifically in writing the agreed or declared value of the property as follows: "The agreed or declared value of the property is specifically stated by the shipper to be not exceeding _____ per _____.

Received, subject to individually determined rates or contracts that have been agreed upon in writing between the carrier and shipper, if applicable, otherwise to the rates, classifications and rules that have been established by the carrier and are available to the shipper, on request, and to all applicable state and federal regulations.

The carrier shall not make delivery of this shipment without payment of freight and all other lawful charges.

Shipper Signature *Jerry Richards*

Shipper Signature/Date

This is to certify that the above named materials are properly classified, packaged, marked and labeled, and are in proper condition for transportation according to the applicable regulations of the DOT.

Jerry Richards 06/12/XX

Trailer Loaded:
☐ By shipper
☑ By Driver

Carrier Signature/Pickup Date
Carrier acknowledges receipt of packages and required placards. Carrier certifies emergency response information was made available and/or carrier has the DOT emergency response guidebook or equivalent documentation in the vehicle. Property described above is received in good order, except as noted.

Santos Padilla 6/12/XX

Distribution: Copy 1 - Accounting; Copy 2 - Shipping; Copy 3- Customer

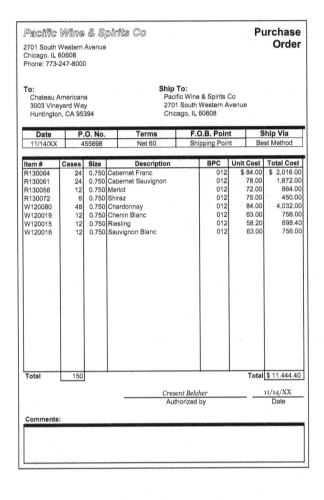

Pacific Wine & Spirits Co

2701 South Western Avenue
Chicago, IL 60608
Phone: 773-247-8000

Purchase Order

To:	Ship To:
Chateau Americana	Pacific Wine & Spirits Co
3003 Vineyard Way	2701 South Western Avenue
Huntington, CA 95394	Chicago, IL 60608

Date	P.O. No.	Terms	F.O.B. Point	Ship Via
11/14/XX	455698	Net 60	Shipping Point	Best Method

Item #	Cases	Size	Description	BPC	Unit Cost	Total Cost
R130064	24	0.750	Cabernet Franc	012	$ 84.00	$ 2,016.00
R130061	24	0.750	Cabernet Sauvignon	012	78.00	1,872.00
R130056	12	0.750	Merlot	012	72.00	864.00
R130072	6	0.750	Shiraz	012	75.00	450.00
W120080	48	0.750	Chardonnay	012	84.00	4,032.00
W120019	12	0.750	Chenin Blanc	012	63.00	756.00
W120015	12	0.750	Riesling	012	58.20	698.40
W120016	12	0.750	Sauvignon Blanc	012	63.00	756.00
Total	**150**				**Total**	**$ 11,444.40**

Cresent Belcher   11/14/XX
Authorized by   Date

Comments:

		CREDIT SALES INVOICE		**Invoice Number:**	**15303**

Chateau Americana, Inc.
3003 Vineyard Way
Huntington, CA 95394
(707)368-8485
CA-NC-67

Invoice Date: 11/20/XX

Credit Terms: Net 60

Sold To:	Ship To:
Pacific Wine & Spirits Co	Pacific Wine & Spirits Co
2701 South Western Avenue	2701 South Western Avenue
Chicago, IL 60608	Chicago, IL 60608

Salesperson	Customer P.O. Number	Customer Number	ABC Number
CEZ	455698	1301	IS48489

Product	Description	Size	Quantity	Cost	Extended
R130064	Cabernet Franc	0.750	288	$ 7.00	$ 2,016.00
R130061	Cabernet Sauvignon	0.750	288	6.50	1,872.00
R130056	Merlot	0.750	144	6.00	864.00
R130072	Shiraz	0.750	72	6.25	450.00
W120080	Chardonnay	0.750	576	7.00	4,032.00
W120019	Chenin Blanc	0.750	144	5.25	756.00
W120015	Riesling	0.750	144	4.85	698.40
W120016	Sauvignon Blanc	0.750	144	5.25	756.00

Grand Total Bottles:	1,800	Grand Total Cost:	$ 11,444.40

Total Cases: 150
Comments:

	Date	11/20/XX
	Invoice Number	15303
	Customer Number	1301

Distribution: Copy 1 - Accounting; Copy 2 - Shipping; Copy 3 - Customer; Copy 4 - Sales

---

Date	11/20/XX	Uniform Bill of Lading		

Ship From		**Bill of Lading Number:**	136249

Name:	*Chateau Americana, Inc.*
Address:	3003 Vineyard Way
City/State/Zip:	Huntington, CA 95394
SID No.:	122448

Carrier Name: *Crossway Deliveries*

Ship To		**Trailer Number:** DDR 7192
Name:	*Pacific Wine & Spirits Co*	
Address:	2701 South Western Avenue	**Serial Number:** 000123123
City/State/Zip:	Chicago, IL 60608	
CID No.:	617493	

Special Instructions:

Freight Charge Terms: (Freight charges are prepaid unless marked otherwise)
Prepaid: ☐   Collect: ☒   3rd Party: ☐
(check box): Master bill of lading with attached underlying bills of lading.

Customer Order Information

Description of Items	Quantity	Weight	Pallet/Slip (circle one)	Additional Shipper Information
Wine	150	5,100	(Y) N	
			Y N	
			Y N	
			Y N	
Grand Total	150	5,100		

COD Amount: $ _____   N/A
Free Terms:
☐ Collect
☐ Prepaid
☐ Customer check acceptable

Note: Liability limitation for loss or damage in this shipment may be applicable. See 49 USC §14706 (c) (1) (A) & (B)

Received, subject to individually determined rates or contracts that have been agreed upon in writing between the carrier and shipper, if applicable, otherwise to the rates, classifications and rules that have been established by the carrier and are available to the shipper, on request, and to all applicable state and federal regulations.

The carrier shall not make delivery of this shipment without payment of freight and all other lawful charges.

Shipper Signature   *Jerry Richards*

Shipper Signature/Date	**Trailer Loaded:**	**Carrier Signature/Pickup Date**
This is to certify that the above named materials are properly classified, packaged, marked and labeled, and are in proper condition for transportation according to the applicable regulations of the DOT.	☐ By shipper ☒ By Driver	Carrier acknowledges receipt of packages and required placards. Carrier certifies emergency response information was made available and/or carrier has the DOT emergency response guidebook or equivalent documentation in the vehicle. **Property described above is received in good order, except as noted.**
Jerry Richards 11/20/XX		*Rich Venditti* 11/20/XX

Distribution: Copy 1 - Accounting; Copy 2 - Shipping; Copy 3- Customer

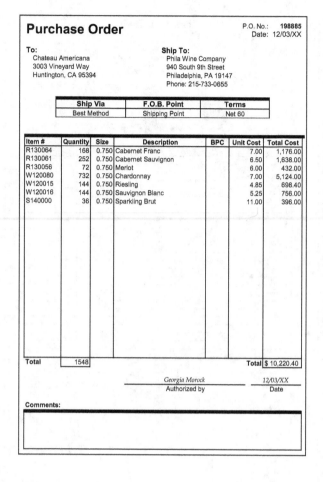

Purchase Order

P.O. No.: **198885**
Date: 12/03/XX

To:
Chateau Americana
3003 Vineyard Way
Huntington, CA 95394

Ship To:
Phila Wine Company
940 South 9th Street
Philadelphia, PA 19147
Phone: 215-733-0655

Ship Via	F.O.B. Point	Terms
Best Method	Shipping Point	Net 60

Item #	Quantity	Size	Description	BPC	Unit Cost	Total Cost
R130064	168	0.750	Cabernet Franc		7.00	1,176.00
R130061	252	0.750	Cabernet Sauvignon		6.50	1,638.00
R130056	72	0.750	Merlot		6.00	432.00
W120080	732	0.750	Chardonnay		7.00	5,124.00
W120015	144	0.750	Riesling		4.85	698.40
W120016	144	0.750	Sauvignon Blanc		5.25	756.00
S140000	36	0.750	Sparkling Brut		11.00	396.00

| Total | 1548 | | | | Total | $ 10,220.40 |

Georgia Morock   12/03/XX
Authorized by   Date

Comments:

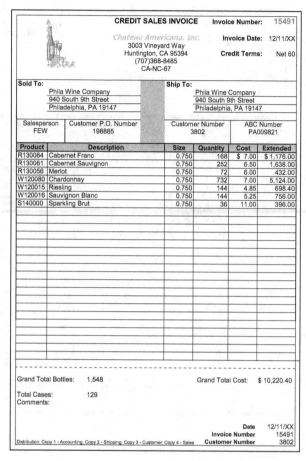

CREDIT SALES INVOICE   Invoice Number: 15491

Chateau Americana, Inc.
3003 Vineyard Way
Huntington, CA 95394   Invoice Date: 12/11/XX
(707)368-8485   Credit Terms: Net 60
CA-NC-67

Sold To:
Phila Wine Company
940 South 9th Street
Philadelphia, PA 19147

Ship To:
Phila Wine Company
940 South 9th Street
Philadelphia, PA 19147

Salesperson FEW	Customer P.O. Number 198885	Customer Number 3802	ABC Number PA009821

Product	Description	Size	Quantity	Cost	Extended
R130064	Cabernet Franc	0.750	168	$ 7.00	$1,176.00
R130061	Cabernet Sauvignon	0.750	252	6.50	1,638.00
R130056	Merlot	0.750	72	6.00	432.00
W120080	Chardonnay	0.750	732	7.00	5,124.00
W120015	Riesling	0.750	144	4.85	698.40
W120016	Sauvignon Blanc	0.750	144	5.25	756.00
S140000	Sparkling Brut	0.750	36	11.00	396.00

Grand Total Bottles: 1,548   Grand Total Cost: $ 10,220.40

Total Cases: 129
Comments:

Date 12/11/XX
Invoice Number 15491
Customer Number 3802

Distribution: Copy 1 - Accounting; Copy 2 - Shipping; Copy 3 - Customer; Copy 4 - Sales

---

Date	12/11/XX	Uniform Bill of Lading	

Ship From   Bill of Lading Number: _____ 136437

Name: *Chateau Americana, Inc.*
Address: *3003 Vineyard Way*
City/State/Zip: *Huntington, CA 95394*
SID No.: *122448*

Carrier Name: *Crossway Deliveries*

Ship To   Trailer Number: *CEF 5824*
Name: *Phila Wine Company*
Address: *940 South 9th Street*   Serial Number: *000360087*
City/State/Zip: *Philadelphia, PA 19147*
CID No.: *463728*

Special Instructions: Freight Charge Terms: (Freight charges are prepaid unless marked otherwise)
Prepaid: ☐ Collect: ☒ 3rd Party: ☐
(check box): Master bill of lading with attached underlying bills of lading.

Customer Order Information

Description of Items	Quantity	Weight	Pallet/Slip (circle one)		Additional Shipper Information
Wine	*129*	*4,386*	(Y)	N	
			Y	N	
			Y	N	
			Y	N	
Grand Total	*129*	*4,386*			

COD Amount: $ _____ N/A
Free Terms:
☐ Collect
☐ Prepaid
☐ Customer check acceptable

Where the rate is dependent on value, shippers are required to state specifically in writing the agreed or declared value of the property as follows: "The agreed or declared value of the property is specifically stated by the shipper to be not exceeding _____ per _____.

Note: Liability limitation for loss or damage in this shipment may be applicable. See 49 USC §14706 (c) (1) (A) & (B)

Received, subject to individually determined rates or contracts that have been agreed upon in writing between the carrier and shipper, if applicable, otherwise to the rates, classifications and rules that have been established by the carrier and are available to the shipper, on request, and to all applicable state and federal regulations.

The carrier shall not make delivery of this shipment without payment of freight and all other lawful charges.

Shipper Signature   *Jerry Richards*

Shipper Signature/Date   Trailer Loaded: Carrier Signature/Pickup Date

This is to certify that the above named materials are properly classified, packaged, marked and labeled, and are in proper condition for transportation according to the applicable regulations of the DOT.

☐ By shipper
☒ By Driver

Carrier acknowledges receipt of packages and required placards. Carrier certifies emergency response information was made available and/or carrier has the DOT emergency response guidebook or equivalent documentation in the vehicle. Property described above is received in good order, except as noted.

Jerry Richards 12/11/XX   *Tom Greer* 12/11/XX

Distribution: Copy 1 - Accounting; Copy 2 - Shipping; Copy 3- Customer

	Customer	Total	Days Old			
Customer	ID	Balance	0 - 60	61 - 120	121 - 180	Over 180
Atlanta Wholesale Wine	1001	$151,696.20	$151,696.20			
Bock Wines and Vines	0501	$210,198.20	$171,946.40	$38,251.80		
Bolliger, Inc.	0701	$163,570.80	$163,570.80			
Pinnacle Wine Company	3201	$184,610.40	$135,978.00	$48,632.40		
Vintage Wine Company	0502	$255,169.80	$207,893.40	$47,276.40		

The Winery at Chateau Americana
Accounts Receivable Aged Trial Balance for Audit Procedure 14*
As of December 31, 20XX

*Abstracted from the Accounts Receivable Aged Trial Balance using exact format of the actual
 Accounts Receivable Aged Trial Balance.

Document 1: Confirmation Letter

Chateau Americana, Inc.
3003 Vineyard Way, Huntington, CA 95394
(707)368-8485

January 2, 20XY

Atlanta Wholesale Wine
275 Spring Street Southwest
Atlanta, GA 30303

Ladies and Gentlemen:

In connection with an audit of the financial statements of Chateau Americana, Inc. as of December 31, 20XX, and for the year then ended, our independent auditors wish to determine whether our records of your indebtedness to us agree with your records. According to our records, your indebtedness to us on December 31, 20XX included the following invoice(s):

Invoice Number	Invoice Date	Amount
15172	11/05/XX	$ 21,890.40
15275	11/17/XX	22,683.60
15331	11/24/XX	27,246.60
15438	12/05/XX	24,078.60
15534	12/16/XX	28,659.00
15644	12/29/XX	27,138.00
Total		$151,696.20

This is neither a request for payment, nor an indication of your total indebtedness to us.

Please confirm whether the information about your indebtedness to us presented above agrees with your records by completing and signing the information below and returning this letter directly to our independent auditors, Boston & Greer, LLP, 1000 Ridge Street, Sacramento, CA, 95814. An addressed envelope is enclosed for your convenience.

Sincerely,

Rob Breeden

Robert Breeden
Chief Financial Officer, Chateau Americana, Inc.

- -

Dear Boston & Greer, LLP:

The above information regarding our indebtedness to Chateau Americana, Inc.

_____ Agrees with our records.
__X__ Does not agree with our records as described below

Exception(s):

Did not receive the shipment related to invoice # 15644 until January 1, 20XY. Our indebtedness to Chateau American was $124,558.20 as of December 31, 20XX.

Name and Title (please print): Blake Conroe, Accounts Payable Clerk

Signature: *Blake Conroe* Date: *1/7/XY*

Document 2: Credit Sales Invoice

CREDIT SALES INVOICE Invoice Number: 15644

Chateau Americana, Inc.
3003 Vineyard Way
Huntington, CA 95394
(707)368-8485
CA-NC-67

Invoice Date: 12/29/XX
Credit Terms: Net 60

Sold To:	Ship To:
Atlanta Wholesale Wine	Atlanta Wholesale Wine
275 Spring Street Southwest	275 Spring Street Southwest
Atlanta, GA 30303	Atlanta, GA 30303

Salesperson MMM	Customer P.O. Number 11332	Customer Number 1001	ABC Number GA3141

Product	Description	Size	Quantity	Cost	Extended
R130064	Cabernet Franc		204	$7.00	$ 1,428.00
R130061	Cabernet Sauvignon		204	6.50	1,326.00
R130056	Merlot		144	6.00	864.00
R130072	Shiraz		144	6.25	900.00
W120080	Chardonnay		1824	7.00	12,768.00
W120019	Chenin Blanc		396	5.25	2,079.00
W120015	Riesling		300	4.85	1,455.00
W120016	Sauvignon Blanc		600	5.25	3,150.00
S140000	Sparkling Brut		288	11.00	3,168.00

Grand Total Bottles: 4,104

Grand Total Cost: $ 27,138.00

Total Cases: 342

Comments:
Rush delivery

Date 12/29/XX
Invoice Number 15644
Customer Number 1001

Distribution: Copy 1 - Accounting; Copy 2 - Shipping; Copy 3 - Customer; Copy 4 - Sales

Document 3: Purchase Order

Purchase Order *Atlanta Wholesale Wine* P.O. No.: **11332**
275 Spring Street Southwest
Atlanta, GA 30303
404-522-3358

To:	Ship To:
Chateau Americana	Atlanta Wholesale Wine
3003 Vineyard Way	275 Spring Street Southwest
Huntington, CA 95394	Atlanta, GA 30303

Date	Terms	F.O.B. Point	Ship Via
12/24/XX	Net 60	Shipping Point	Best Method

Item #	Cases	Size	Description	Unit Cost	Total Cost
R130064	17	750ML	Cabernet Franc	$ 84.00	$ 1,428.00
R130061	17	750ML	Cabernet Sauvignon	78.00	1,326.00
R130056	12	750ML	Merlot	72.00	864.00
R130072	12	750ML	Shiraz	75.00	900.00
W120080	152	750ML	Chardonnay	84.00	12,768.00
W120019	33	750ML	Chenin Blanc	63.00	2,079.00
W120015	25	750ML	Riesling	58.20	1,455.00
W120016	50	750ML	Sauvignon Blanc	63.00	3,150.00
S140000	24	750ML	Sparkling Brut	132.00	3,168.00

Total $ 27,138.00

Jean Kalicki 12/24/XX
Authorized by Date

Comments:

Document 4: Uniform Bill of Lading

Date 12/29/XX	Uniform Bill of Lading

Ship From

Name: *Chateau Americana, Inc.*
Address: *3003 Vineyard Way*
City/State/Zip: *Huntington, CA 95394*
SID No.: *122448*

Bill of Lading Number: 136590

Carrier Name: *EA Shipping*

Ship To
Name: *Atlanta Wholesale Wine*
Address: *275 Spring Street Southwest*
City/State/Zip: *Atlanta, GA 30303*
CID No.: *002996*

Trailer Number: *4578 CAL*
Serial Number: *000111789*

Special Instructions:

Freight Charge Terms: (Freight charges are prepaid unless marked otherwise)
Prepaid: ☐ Collect: ☒ 3rd Party: ☐
☐ (check box): Master bill of lading with attached underlying bills of lading.

Customer Order Information

Description of Items	Quantity	Weight	Pallet/Slip (circle one)	Additional Shipper Information
Wine	342	11,628	Ⓨ N	
			Y N	
			Y N	
			Y N	
Grand Total	342	11,628		

COD Amount: $ N/A
Free Terms:
☐ Collect
☐ Prepaid
☐ Customer check acceptable

Where the rate is dependent on value, shippers are required to state specifically in writing the agreed or declared value of the property. "The agreed or declared value of the property is specifically stated by the shipper to be not exceeding _____ per _____."

Note: Liability limitation for loss or damage in this shipment may be applicable. See 49 USC §14706 (c) (1) (A) & (B)

Received, subject to individually determined rates or contracts that have been agreed upon in writing between the carrier and shipper, if applicable, otherwise to the rates, classifications and rules that have been established by the carrier and are available to the shipper, on request, and to all applicable state and federal regulations.

The carrier shall not make delivery of this shipment without payment of and all other lawful charges.

Shipper Signature _____ Jerry Richards

Shipper Signature/Date

This is to certify that the above named materials are properly classified, packaged, marked and labeled, and are in proper condition for transportation according to the applicable regulations of the DOT.

Jerry Richards 12/29/XX

Trailer Loaded:
☐ By shipper
☒ By Driver

Carrier Signature/Pickup Date

Carrier acknowledges receipt of packages and required placards. Carrier certifies emergency response information was made available and/or carrier has the DOT emergency response guidebook or equivalent documentation in the vehicle. Property described above is received in good order, except as noted.

Sam Souza 12/29/XX

Distribution: Copy 1 - Accounting; Copy 2 - Shipping; Copy 3- Customer

Chateau Americana, Inc.
3003 Vineyard Way, Huntington, CA 95394
(707)368-8485

January 2, 20XY

Bock Wines and Vines
Pier 19, The Embarcadero
San Francisco, CA 94111

Ladies and Gentlemen:

In connection with an audit of the financial statements of Chateau Americana, Inc. as of December 31, 20XX, and for the year then ended, our independent auditors wish to determine whether our records of your indebtedness to us agree with your records. According to our records, your indebtedness to us on December 31, 20XX included the following invoice(s):

Invoice Number	Invoice Date	Amount
14944	10/09/XX	$ 18,501.00
15072	10/24/XX	19,750.80
15158	11/03/XX	19,337.60
15252	11/14/XX	20,206.80
15335	11/24/XX	23,826.00
15406	12/01/XX	22,042.80
15465	12/08/XX	24,682.80
15551	12/18/XX	30,303.60
15619	12/26/XX	31,546.80
Total		$210,198.20

This is neither a request for payment, nor an indication of your total indebtedness to us.

Please confirm whether the information about your indebtedness to us presented above agrees with your records by completing and signing the information below and returning this letter directly to our independent auditors, Boston & Greer, LLP, 1000 Ridge Street, Sacramento, CA, 95814. An addressed envelope is enclosed for your convenience.

Sincerely,

Rob Breeden

Robert Breeden
Chief Financial Officer, Chateau Americana, Inc.

- -

Dear Boston & Greer, LLP:

The above information regarding our indebtedness to Chateau Americana, Inc.

    _____ Agrees with our records.
    __X__ Does not agree with our records as described below

Exception(s):

Mailed check on 12/30/20XX for $18,501.00 (check number 25386), our outstanding balance was $191,697.20 on 12/31/20XX.

Name and Title (please print): Diana Meiburg, Controller

Signature: *Diana Meiburg*   Date: *1/9/20XY*

Grand Total Bottles:	2,640	Grand Total Cost:	$ 18,501.00
Total Cases:	220		
Comments:			
Rush delivery			

	Date	10/09/XX
	Invoice Number	14944
	Customer Number	0501

Distribution: Copy 1 - Accounting; Copy 2 - Shipping; Copy 3 - Customer

---

Bank of Huntington   Customer Receipt

All items credited subject to verification, collection, and conditions of the Rules and Regulations of this Bank and as otherwise provided by law. Payments are accepted when credit is applied to outstanding balances and not upon issuance of this receipt. Transactions received after the Bank's posted cut-off time or Saturday, Sunday, and Bank Holidays, are dated and considered received as of the next business day.

Please retain this receipt until you receive your account statement.

00406 018 057167 01-03-XY 16:52 DEP BUS
640665135 000000000739601109 $131,677.20

86-15-2007C 06-2001

Cash Receipt Summary   # 5719

Chateau Americana
3003 Vineyard Way
Huntington, CA 95394

Date : *1/2/XY*
Preparer 1 Initial: *MSB*
Preparer 2 Initial: *GLH*

Customer/Description	Ref./Customer #	Invoice #	Amount
Bock Wines and Vines	0501	14944	$ 18,501.00
Glazer's Distributors of Ohio	3502	15163	12,365.40
Louis Carufel Wine Co	0503	15154	16,255.20
Bacchus Wine Wholesale Distribution	0902	15175	13,203.60
Prestige Wine Cellars	4301	15192	10,996.20
American Vineyards	3501	15129	12,533.40
Veritas Distributors Inc	2201	15189	14,125.80
Fine Wine Selection Company	0301	15170	11,164.20
Mountain Wine Distributing Company	0601	15121	13,581.60
World Vintage Imports Inc	2101	15153	8,950.80
Total			$ 131,677.20

Chateau Americana, Inc.
3003 Vineyard Way, Huntington, CA 95394
(707)368-8485

January 2, 20XY

Bolliger, Inc.
88 Viaduct Road
Stamford, CT 06907

Ladies and Gentlemen:

In connection with an audit of the financial statements of Chateau Americana, Inc. as of December 31, 20XX, and for the year then ended, our independent auditors wish to determine whether our records of your indebtedness to us agree with your records. According to our records, your indebtedness to us on December 31, 20XX included the following invoice(s):

Invoice Number	Invoice Date	Amount
15156	11/03/XX	$ 23,532.00
15233	11/12/XX	25,116.00
15308	11/21/XX	29,407.20
15431	12/04/XX	23,710.80
15542	12/17/XX	30,110.40
15618	12/26/XX	31,694.40

Total $163,570.80

This is neither a request for payment, nor an indication of your total indebtedness to us.

Please confirm whether the information about your indebtedness to us presented above agrees with your records by completing and signing the information below and returning this letter directly to our independent auditors, Boston & Greer, LLP, 1000 Ridge Street, Sacramento, CA, 95814. An addressed envelope is enclosed for your convenience.

Sincerely,

Rob Breeden

Robert Breeden
Chief Financial Officer, Chateau Americana, Inc.

– –

Dear Boston & Greer, LLP:

The above information regarding our indebtedness to Chateau Americana, Inc.

   _X_ Agrees with our records.
   _____ Does not agree with our records as described below

Exception(s):

   N/A

Name and Title (please print):   Arnoldo Tucci, Accounts Payable Manager

Signature: *Arnoldo Tucci*   Date: _1/13/XY_

Chateau Americana, Inc.
3003 Vineyard Way, Huntington, CA 95394
(707)368-8485

January 2, 20XY

Pinnacle Wine Company
345 Underhill Blvd.
Syosset, New York 11791

Ladies and Gentlemen:

In connection with an audit of the financial statements of Chateau Americana, Inc. as of December 31, 20XX, and for the year then ended, our independent auditors wish to determine whether our records of your indebtedness to us agree with your records. According to our records, your indebtedness to us on December 31, 20X included the following invoice(s):

Invoice Number	Invoice Date	Amount
15047	10/21/XX	$ 24,129.60
15132	10/31/XX	24,502.80
15235	11/12/XX	26,086.80
15312	11/21/XX	29,254.80
15403	12/01/XX	23,710.80
15525	12/15/XX	26,086.80
15612	12/26/XX	30,838.80
Total		$184,610.40

This is neither a request for payment, nor an indication of your total indebtedness to us.

Please confirm whether the information about your indebtedness to us presented above agrees with your records by completing and signing the information below and returning this letter directly to our independent auditors, Boston & Greer, LLP, 1000 Ridge Street, Sacramento, CA, 95814. An addressed envelope is enclosed for your convenience.

Sincerely,

Rob Breeden

Robert Breeden
Chief Financial Officer, Chateau Americana, Inc.

- -

Dear Boston & Greer, LLP:

The above information regarding our indebtedness to Chateau Americana, Inc.

   __X__ Agrees with our records.
   _____ Does not agree with our records as described below

Exception(s):

Name and Title (please print):   Maurice Vasser, Assistant Controller

Signature: *Maurice Vasser*   Date: *1/14/20XY*

Chateau Americana, Inc.
3003 Vineyard Way, Huntington, CA 95394
(707)368-8485

January 2, 20XY

Vintage Wine Company
2650 Commerce Way
Los Angeles, Ca 90040

Ladies and Gentlemen:

In connection with an audit of the financial statements of Chateau Americana, Inc. as of December 31, 20XX, and for the year then ended, our independent auditors wish to determine whether our records of your indebtedness to us agree with your records. According to our records, your indebtedness to us on December 31, 20XX included the following invoice(s):

Invoice Number	Invoice Date	Amount
15038	10/20/XX	$ 22,206.00
15123	10/30/XX	25,070.40
15217	11/10/XX	26,769.60
15299	11/19/XX	27,058.80
15337	11/24/XX	29,340.00
15440	12/05/XX	27,598.80
15488	12/11/XX	28,096.80
15550	12/18/XX	30,463.20
15611	12/26/XX	38,566.20
Total		$255,169.80

This is neither a request for payment, nor an indication of your total indebtedness to us.

Please confirm whether the information about your indebtedness to us presented above agrees with your records by completing and signing the information below and returning this letter directly to our independent auditors, Boston & Greer, LLP, 1000 Ridge Street, Sacramento, CA, 95814. An addressed envelope is enclosed for your convenience.

Sincerely,

Rob Breeden

Robert Breeden
Chief Financial Officer, Chateau Americana, Inc.

- -

Dear Boston & Greer, LLP:

The above information regarding our indebtedness to Chateau Americana, Inc.

_____ Agrees with our records.
__X__ Does not agree with our records as described below

Exception(s):

Invoice # 15611 included an over shipment of 70 cases of Chardonnay (Product # W120080) at $84 a case. The 70 cases were shipped back to Chateau Americana on 12/29/XX. Our records indicated that our indebtedness to Chateau American was $249,289.80 on December 31, 20XX.

Name and Title (please print):   Rachel Parks, Controller

Signature: *Rachel Parks*   Date: *1/15/XY*

Credit Memo

Chateau Americana, Inc.
3003 Vineyard Way
Huntington, CA 95394

Phone: (707)368-8485

Credit Memo: **2896**	
Date: 1/5/XY	**Sales Person:** WAB
Customer Number: 0502	**Customer PO No:** 287654
Amount Net: $5,880.00	

Credit To: Vintage Wine Company
Comments:

Over-shipped customer 70 cases of Chardonnay

		Price	
Item # / Description	**Quantity**	**Unit Price**	**Amount**
W120080 / Chardonnay	840	$7.00	$5,880.00

Customer Name:		Credit Amount:	$5,880.00
Vintage Wine Company			

Chateau Americana
3003 Vineyard Way
Huntington, CA 95394
Phone: (707)368-8485

Credit Date:	1/5/XY
Credit Memo #:	**2896**
Customer Number:	0502

Distribution: Copy 1 - Accounting; Copy 2 - Customer

Receiving Report

Date Received: *12/31/XX*
Receiving Report #: **17263**

Received From	**Purchase Order #**
Vintage Wine Company	Credit Sales Invoice # 15611
Freight Carrier	**Received by**
West Cost Shipping	BH

Quantity	Item #	Size	Description
840	W120080	0.750	70 Cases of Chardonnay

Condition:

Excellent

Distribution: Copy 1 - Accounting; Copy 2 - Purchasing; Copy 3 - Receiving

COMPLETING THE AUDIT:
The Winery At Chateau Americana

LEARNING OBJECTIVES

After completing and discussing this case, you should be able to:

- Understand and identify audit procedures to detect contingent liabilities and commitments
- Understand and identify audit procedures to detect subsequent events
- Understand and evaluate information relevant to the assessment of the going concern assumption
- Evaluate and recognize potential limitations of responses to letters of inquiry sent to legal counsel
- Identify information that must be included in a management representation letter
- Understand and evaluate a summary of unadjusted differences schedule
- Prepare an audit report that is appropriate in light of client circumstances
- Understand the required communications with those charged with governance

INTRODUCTION

Your firm's first audit of Chateau Americana is drawing to a close and your partner, Claire Helton, has just informed you that the next couple of days will be devoted to wrapping up the engagement. She plans to present the firm's audit report to the winery's chief financial officer next week; however, there are a number of audit procedures that remain open on this year's audit program and must be completed prior to next week's meeting.

Several client interviews were conducted by Elise Simpson, another senior auditor assigned to the engagement. You will find transcripts of these interviews and the accompanying documents useful in completing the open items.

INTERVIEW TRANSCRIPTS

Elise: Good morning Edward. I have several questions to ask you to help with completing our audit. Are you aware of any contingent liabilities that should be disclosed in the financial statements?

Edward: You've already received the letter from our attorney regarding the lawsuit filed by a former employee. We hope to resolve the suit in the very near future. I'm not aware of any other lawsuits or contingencies.

Elise: Have there been similar suits filed against your company in the past?

Edward: No, this is the first employee-initiated suit of this type. We've made every attempt to maintain excellent working conditions and relationships with our employees.

Elise: Does the company have any sales or purchase contracts?

Edward: We don't have any sales contracts, but we do have several purchase contracts that we use to secure our supply of grapes. We've maintained purchase agreements with the same growers for the past 12 years and we've never been disappointed by either the quality of their product or the contract terms. Under the terms of these agreements we are required to purchase a predetermined amount of grapes at prices based on existing market conditions, although some contracts establish minimum purchase prices.

Elise: I suppose such contracts can be beneficial or detrimental.

Edward: That's precisely why we're so methodical in establishing sales projections that we use to calculate our inventory requirements.

Elise: Does the company have any other commitments, such as equipment or building leases?

Edward: I personally own some of the production equipment that I lease to the company. I believe Rob provided a copy of the lease agreement to someone on the audit team. There are no other leases or commitments of any type.

Elise: My last question relates to subsequent events. Are you aware of any event that has occurred since the balance sheet date that requires either adjustment to or disclosure in the financial statements? For example, have there been any changes in the company's capital stock or long-term debt, or any unusual adjustments since the end of the year?

Edward: Rob and I met with representatives from the financial institutions that we have loans with several weeks ago to discuss the possibility of restructuring our long term debt. Given the recent downward trends in interest rates, we decided to attempt to secure a lower rate and shorter repayment terms for our debt. Although we're still negotiating, we expect to reach an agreement within the next week or two.

Otherwise, there have been no changes to our debt or capital structure and there have definitely been no unusual adjustments to our financial statements.

◆ ◆

After meeting with Edward, Elise met with Rob Breeden, CA's chief financial officer.

Elise:	Hi Rob. Thanks for meeting with me this morning. I need to talk with you about several issues so that we can finalize our audit in time for your and Claire's meeting next week. First, are you aware of any contingent liabilities that should be disclosed in the financial statements?
Rob:	No, our only current litigation relates to a lawsuit filed by a former employee. We're working very hard through our attorney to resolve the suit.
Elise:	Are you likely to offer a settlement to the individual?
Rob:	I can't say with any certainty what we'll do. Our attorney is still in the process of researching the case and formulating a position for us. We've never had a suit such as this brought against our company, so we're in new territory. I can tell you that Edward feels very strongly about resolving the case as quickly as possible and keeping it out of the press.
Elise:	Could you tell me a little about the case?
Rob:	William Simmons worked for the winery for six years prior to the accident. He was a dependable and competent employee according to his supervisor. As I understand it, William was injured while he was repairing one of our large storage tanks. The insurance report states that he fell when his safety harness broke. He sustained several broken ribs, a broken arm and a broken leg. He contends that the company was negligent in maintaining the equipment. We're not convinced that he was using it properly.
Elise:	Do you have any idea of what the maximum settlement could be?
Rob:	The suit seeks damages of $500,000, or almost 20 times the former employee's prior year's earnings.
Elise:	Turning to a different subject now. Tell me about any sales or purchase contracts.
Rob:	We don't enter into sales contracts. However, because we rely on outside growers for almost 75% of our grapes, we do contract with growers to ensure a flow of grapes. We've had agreements with a number of the same growers for many years. Based on my experience, the contract terms are relatively favorable. The greatest benefit to us is that we're assured a flow of inventory.
Elise:	Do the agreements set minimum prices?
Rob:	We obviously use these contracts to ensure a continuous source of grapes. While most of the contracts call for prices to be based on market conditions, several establish minimum purchase prices. However, we've

been able to negotiate prices that we believe still provide a great deal of protection for us.

Elise: Edward mentioned that you are very careful in forecasting your grape needs. Who is responsible for the forecasting process?

Rob: I oversee the process. Our calculations are based on sales projections developed by our sales manager, Susan Platt. She has more years of experience in the wine industry than most of us and has always done a very competent job for us. After Susan finishes her calculations she and I meet with Taylor, the company's vice president of marketing, to go over the numbers.

Elise: Does the company have any commitments?

Rob: We lease certain production equipment from Edward. I think I may have mentioned that to you when were discussing related party transactions. Our total monthly lease payments are approximately $9,000. We have no other leases or commitments.

Elise: Have there been any subsequent events since the end of the year? Also, have there been changes in the company's capital stock or long-term debt, or any unusual adjustments since the end of the year?

Rob: You may be interested to know that Edward and I have had several meetings with our creditors in recent weeks to negotiate changes in our loan terms. I have been talking to Edward about our need to take advantage of the recent interest rates drops. Edward finally has agreed to pursue a shorter payback period in hopes of extinguishing our debt earlier than originally planned.

Elise: Have you reached an agreement with the financial institutions?

Rob: Nothing definite at this point. We're in the process of working out the details. I'm hopeful that we'll agree on new terms within the next several weeks.

◆◆

The following documents are relevant to the completion of your firm's audit of Chateau Americana's financial statements and may be found on the following pages:

1. Draft of the current year's financial statements
2. Summary of Unadjusted Differences (prepared by the audit team)
3. Attorney's Response to Audit Inquiry Letter
4. Minutes from the company's Board of Directors meetings

The Winery at Chateau Americana, Inc.
Balance Sheets as of December 31, 20XX – 20XV
(In Thousands)

Draft - for Internal Use Only

ASSETS

	20XX	20XW	20XV
CURRENT ASSETS			
Cash	$ 3,005	$ 2,992	$ 3,281
Accounts receivable (net of allowance)	5,241	4,816	3,703
Investments	3,095	2,081	2,294
Production inventories	11,578	10,407	9,107
Finished goods inventories	4,015	3,902	3,567
Prepaid expenses	142	85	69
Total Current Assets	27,076	$ 24,283	$ 22,021
PROPERTY, PLANT & EQUIPMENT	30,230	28,135	27,612
Less accumulated depreciation	15,277	14,096	13,185
Net Property, Plant & Equipment	14,953	14,039	14,427
TOTAL ASSETS	$ 42,029	$ 38,322	$ 36,448

LIABILITIES AND SHAREHOLDERS' EQUITY

	20XX	20XW	20XV
CURRENT LIABILITIES			
Accounts payable	$ 4,988	$ 3,683	$ 2,221
Accrued expenses	599	569	640
Notes payable	813	654	891
Current portion of long term debt	410	525	464
Payroll taxes withheld and payable	100	95	96
Federal income tax payable	172	157	134
Total Current Liabilities	7,082	5,683	4,446
LONG TERM DEBT	7,229	6,918	7,983
TOTAL LIABILITIES	14,311	12,601	12,429
SHAREHOLDERS' EQUITY			
Common stock (No par value, 5,000,000			
shares authorized, 45,000 shares issued)	90	90	90
Additional paid-in capital	3,567	3,567	3,567
Retained earnings	24,061	22,064	20,362
Total Shareholders' Equity	27,718	25,721	24,019
TOTAL LIABILITIES AND SHAREHOLDERS' EQUITY	$ 42,029	$ 38,322	$ 36,448

Draft - for Internal Use Only

The Winery at Chateau Americana, Inc.
Statements of Income for Years Ended December 31, 20XX – 20XV
(In Thousands)

Draft - for Internal Use Only

	20XX	20XW	20XV
Sales	$ 21,945	$ 20,189	$ 18,170
Cost of goods sold	11,543	10,525	9,777
Gross profit	10,402	9,664	8,393
Selling, general and administrative expenses	7,017	6,824	6,218
Operating income	3,386	2,840	2,175
Interest expense	360	211	257
Provision for income taxes	1,028	927	483
Net income	$ 1,997	$ 1,702	$ 1,435

Draft - for Internal Use Only

Summary of Unadjusted Differences

Client:	The Winery at Chateau Americana, Inc.
Year ended:	December 31, 20XX

Reference:	*CA-4*
Prepared by:	*WJ, 3-2-XY*
Approved:	

Audit Schedule Reference	Description of Misstatement	Type of Misstatement	Total Amount	Possible Misstatements Overstatements / (Understatements)			
				Current Assets	Noncurrent Assets	Current Liabilities	Income Before Taxes
R-210	Write-off of customer account receivable	P	($13,488)	($13,488)			
E-210	Unrecorded accounts payable	P	61,917	(31,200)	($20,717)	($61,917)	10,000
I-210	Unrecorded capital acquisitions	A	48,610	48,610	(48,610)		
I-210	Misstatement in depreciation expense	A	13,368	13,368	13,368		13,368
				$	$	$	$

	Possible Overstatement (Understatement)	Materiality
Total Assets	$	$1,050,725
Income Before Taxes	$	$99,850

Conclusion:

McKenna, Harmon, & Jacobs
First Union Square Place
1450 California Avenue
Napa, CA 41008

CA-201
PBC/AG
3/15/XY

March 12, 20XY

Boston & Greer, LLP
1000 Ridge Street
Sacramento, CA, 95814

Re: The Winery at Chateau Americana, Inc.

Dear Sirs:

By letter dated, March 1, 20XY, Mr. Rob Breeden, Chief Financial Officer of The Winery at Chateau Americana, Inc., (the "Company") has requested us to furnish you with certain information in connection with your examination of the accounts of the Company as of December 31, 20XX.

While this firm represents the Company on a regular basis, our engagement has been limited to specific matters as to which we were consulted by the Company.

Subject to the foregoing and to the last paragraph of this letter, we advise you that since January 1, 20XX we have not been engaged to give substantive attention to, or represent the Company in connection with, material loss contingencies coming within the scope of clause (a) of Paragraph 5 of the Statement of Policy referred to in the last paragraph of this letter, except as follows:

> On November 21, 20XX, a suit was filed against The Winery at Chateau Americana, Inc. by a former employee who is seeking damages for injuries sustained while employed by the Company. The suit alleges that William Simmons (the "Employee") was injured as a result of the Company's negligent maintenance of workplace safety equipment as required by the Occupational Safety & Health Administration. In addition, the suit claims that Simmons was not instructed in the proper use of the safety equipment as required by applicable federal and state laws. According to the suit, Simmons was performing routine maintenance on one of the Company's wine storage tanks when a safety harness he was wearing failed. The fall resulted in a loss of work time, hospitalization, and significant physical therapy.

> In preparation of providing this letter to you, we have reviewed the merits of the claim against the Company. After careful consideration, we are unable to express an opinion as to the merits of the litigation at this time. The Company believes there is absolutely no merit to the litigation.

The information set forth herein is as of March 12, 20XY, the date on which we commenced our internal review procedures for purposes of preparing this response, except as otherwise noted, and we disclaim any undertaking to advise you of changes which thereafter may be brought to our attention.

This response is limited by, and in general accordance with, the ABA Statement of Policy Regarding Lawyers' Responses to Auditors' Requests for Information (December 1975); without limiting the generality of the foregoing, the limitations set forth in such Statement on the scope and use of this response (Paragraphs 2 and 7) are specifically incorporated herein by reference, and any description herein of any "loss contingencies" is qualified in its entirety by Paragraph 5 of the Statement and the accompany Commentary (which is an integral part of the Statement). Consistent with the last sentence of Paragraph 6 of the ABA Statement of Policy and pursuant to the Company's request, this will confirm as correct the Company's understanding as set forth in its audit inquiry letter to us that whenever, in the course of performing legal services for the Company with respect to a matter recognized to involve an unasserted possible claim or assessment that may call for financial statement disclosure, we have formed a professional conclusion that the Company must disclose or consider disclosure concerning such possible claim or assessment, we, as a matter of professional responsibility to the Company, will so advise the Company and will consult with the Company concerning the question of such disclosure and the applicable requirements of Statement of Financial Accounting Standards No. 5.

Very truly yours,

McKenna, Harmon, & Jacobs

Napa, CA

The Winery at Chateau Americana, Inc.

CA-203
PBC/AG
3/05/XY

Board of Directors Meeting
Minutes – March 3, 20XY

The quarterly meeting of the Board of Directors of The Winery at Chateau Americana, Inc. was held at the Company's offices on Wednesday, March 3, 20XY. Mr. Edward Summerfield, Chairman of the Board, called the meeting to order at 9:30 a.m. Eastern Standard Time.

Present at the meeting:

Mr. Edward Summerfield, Chairman of the Board
Ms. Taylor Summerfield, Vice President of Marketing and Member of the Board
Mrs. Charlotte Summerfield, Member of the Board
Mr. Rob Breeden, Chief Financial Officer and Member of the Board
Mr. Bill Jameson, Member of the Board
Ms. Susan Martinez, Member of the Board
Mr. Terrence Dillard, Member of the Board
Mr. Harry West, Outside Legal Counsel (Present only for discussion of pending litigation)

Action Items

1. **Approval of the Minutes**. On a motion duly made and seconded, the Board approved the minutes as distributed of the meeting of Wednesday, December 3, 20XX.

2. **Creation of Committees**. As Chairman of the Board, Mr. Summerfield recommended that the Board establish an Audit Committee. Mr. Summerfield stated that the Company's audit firm had suggested that establishing such a committee would be beneficial to the Company in improving its corporate governance structure.

   On a motion duly made and seconded, the Board adopted the following resolution:

   Resolved, That the Board accepts the Chairman's recommendation to establish an Audit Committee effective as soon as such a committee can be formed.

3. **Nomination and Election of Committee Members**. Mr. Terrence Dillard nominated Ms. Susan Martinez to be the Chair of the Audit Committee and nominated Mr. Bill Jameson and Mrs. Charlotte Summerfield to be members of the Committee.

   On a motion duly made and seconded, the Board adopted the following resolutions:

Resolved, That the Board elects Ms. Susan Martinez as Chair of the Audit Committee and Mr. Bill Jameson and Mrs. Charlotte Summerfield as members of the Committee for a term of one year that shall begin immediately and that shall conclude at the close of the March 20XZ quarterly Board meeting; and

Resolved Further, That the Board directs Ms. Martinez to adopt such practices as may be appropriate to assist the Committee in fulfilling its corporate governance responsibilities. The Committee shall meet no less than two times per year immediately preceding regularly scheduled quarterly Board meetings. Such requirement shall not be construed as limiting the Committee's prerogative to meet more frequently. Further, the Board understands the Committee will meet privately with the Company's auditor to discuss any matters it deems appropriate.

4. **Report on Pending Litigation – Confidential and Proprietary** – Executive Session. A confidential and proprietary supplemental issue paper was distributed at the meeting. Mr. Harry West, partner at McKenna, Harmon, & Jacobs, provided an update regarding the status of the lawsuit filed by William Simmons against the Company. Mr. West recommended that the matter be discussed in Executive Session because this item is about pending litigation matters that are subject to attorney-client privilege.

   On a motion duly made and seconded, the Board adopted the following resolution:

   Resolved, That the Board determines that discussion of an update on pending litigation to which the Company is a party shall be conducted in Executive Session.

Information Items

1. **Restructuring of Long-term Debt**. Mr. Rob Breeden reported that he and Mr. Summerfield have had several meetings with representatives of financial institutions from whom the Company has borrowed funds to discuss renegotiating the current terms of the Company's debt. Although no agreement has been reached, Mr. Breeden stated that he believes the Company will be able to successfully renegotiate debt terms with all related financial institutions.

2. **Update on New Accounting Firm**. Mr. Rob Breeden informed the Board that the Company has been very pleased with the service provided by the recently appointed firm of Boston & Greer, LLP. Mr. Breeden stated that he anticipates receiving the firm's audit report on the Company's financial statements in the coming week. Mr. Jameson inquired whether the firm had identified any significant accounting matters during the course of the audit. Mr. Breeden stated that no significant matters had been identified.

There being no further business, Mr. Summerfield adjourned the meeting at 11:25 a.m. Eastern Standard Time.

REQUIREMENTS

Completing an audit is a challenging process that requires auditors to make a number of critically important decisions. The following questions relate to some of these issues. You should answer these questions prior to completing the "open" audit procedures on the audit program.

1. ASC Topic 450 - *Contingences*, (formerly SFAS No. 5 - *Accounting for Contingencies*) prescribes how companies must treat contingent liabilities in various circumstances. The likelihood that a contingency will arise in any given situation may be considered as probable, reasonably possible, or remote. If an auditor believes that an attorney's response is ambiguous as to the possible outcome of pending litigation, how may an auditor obtain evidence to assess the need for a possible accrual of a loss contingency or disclosure of the matter in the notes to the financial statements? You may wish to refer to SAS No. 12, *Inquiry of a Client's Lawyer Concerning Litigation, Claims, and Assessments*, for help in answering this question.

2. Describe three to five audit procedures that auditors commonly perform to search for contingencies.

3. SAS No. 59, *The Auditor's Consideration of an Entity's Ability to Continue as a Going Concern*, requires auditors to perform an evaluation of an entity's ability to continue as a going concern as part of each audit. Describe several audit procedures that may be used in the auditor's evaluation of going concern. What audit documentation is required if an auditor concludes there is substantial doubt about an entity's ability to continue as a going concern?

4. Generally accepted auditing standards require auditors to obtain written representations from management as part of each audit. To what extent should an auditor rely solely on a client's written representations? At what point in the audit should a representation letter be obtained and as of what date should the client make the representations? What are the implications of management's refusal to provide requested representations?

5. Claire Helton, the engagement partner has been very impressed with your work on Chateau Americana. As a consequence, she has asked you to identify the appropriate audit report for the company. Assuming that each of the following situations is independent from the others, determine the type of audit report which is most appropriate.

    a. Assume that subsequent to year-end, but before issuance of the audit report that one of Chateau Americana's customers filed bankruptcy. The customer's year-end account receivable was $50,750, an immaterial amount. Chateau Americana's CFO indicates that he neither wants to write-off the customer's account, nor record a specific reserve.

    b. Assume the litigation discussed in the case is settled subsequent to year-end for $200,000. The financial statements for the year ended 12/31/20XX did not include a loss accrual. The company does not want to include disclosure regarding the settlement in the financial statements.

c. The company renegotiates certain terms associated with its long term debt subsequent to year-end. The new terms are more favorable than the previous terms, but the principal amount of the outstanding debt did not change as a consequence of the renegotiation. No disclosure is being provided in the financial statements.

d. A flood destroys one-third of the company's vineyard shortly after year-end. The company is currently attempting to secure access to more grapes from the open market. While the company had some insurance on its vineyards, it appears likely that the company will not be indemnified for the full market value of its loss. The value of the lost inventory is material to the financial statements. Management does not intend to include a footnote in the financial statements.

6. Subsequent to year-end, Chateau Americana's board of directors passed a resolution to establish an audit committee. Does this action require any response by your audit team? Describe matters that your firm may discuss with such a committee in future years. Is your audit team required to have such discussions with Chateau Americana's audit committee?

The Winery at Chateau Americana
Partial Audit Program for Completing the Audit

For the Year Ended December 31, 20XX

	Reference:	_CA-100_
	Prepared by:	_AG_
	Date:	_3/15/XY_
	Reviewed by:	

Audit Procedures	Initial	Date	A/S Ref.
1. Request the client to send letters of inquiry to attorneys from whom the client has obtained legal services from during the year.	_AG_	_3/15/XY_	_CA-201_
2. Review the response received from the client's attorney for information related to contingencies. Document issues related to ongoing or pending litigation.			_CA-202_
3. Obtain a copy of the minutes of all meetings of the board of directors subsequent to year end.	_AG_	_3/05/XY_	_CA-203_
4. Review the minutes of the board of directors meeting for subsequent events affecting the current year financial statements. Note items for follow-up during next year's audit.			_CA-204_
5. Complete the Summary of Unadjusted Differences. Conclude whether the financial statements are fairly stated in all material respects.			_CA-4_
6. Prepare a memo to summarize your assessment of the validity of the going concern assumption for Chateau Americana.			_CA-205_
7. Document matters to be included in the current year's management representation letter.			_CA-206_

The Winery at Chateau Americana
Review of Attorneys Letters
For the Year Ended December 31, 20XX

Reference:	*CA-202*
Prepared by:	
Date:	
Reviewed by:	

Matters related to ongoing litigation:

Matters related to pending litigation:

The Winery at Chateau Americana	Reference:	*CA-204*
Review of Minutes of the Board of Directors Meetings	Prepared by:	
For the Year Ended December 31, 20XX	Date:	
	Reviewed by:	

Notes regarding subsequent events affecting the current year financial statements:

Planning notes regarding next year's audit:

The Winery at Chateau Americana
Assessment of Going Concern Assumption
For the Year Ended December 31, 20XX

Reference: *CA-205*
Prepared by: _____
Date: _____
Reviewed by: _____

Comments:

The Winery at Chateau Americana
Matters for Management Representation Letter
For the Year Ended December 31, 20XX

Reference: _CA-206_
Prepared by: _____
Date: _____
Reviewed by: _____

Matters to be included in the current year management represent letter: